Strengthening Science at the U.S. Environmental Protection Agency

Research-Management and Peer-Review Practices

Committee on Research and Peer Review in EPA

Board on Environmental Studies and Toxicology

Commission on Geosciences, Environment, and Resources

Commission on Life Sciences

National Research Council

NATIONAL ACADEMY PRESS
Washington, D.C.

NATIONAL ACADEMY PRESS   2101 Constitution Ave., N.W.   Washington, D.C. 20418

NOTICE: The project that is the subject of this report was approved by the Governing Board of the National Research Council, whose members are drawn from the councils of the National Academy of Sciences, the National Academy of Engineering, and the Institute of Medicine. The members of the committee responsible for the report were chosen for their special competences and with regard for appropriate balance.

This project was supported by Contract No. 68-W4-0044 between the National Academy of Sciences and the U.S. Environmental Protection Agency and by endowment funds of the National Academy of Sciences. Any opinions, findings, conclusions, or recommendations expressed in this publication are those of the author(s) and do not necessarily reflect the views of the U.S. Environmental Protection Agency.

International Standard Book Number 0-309-07127-5

Additional copies of this report are available from:

National Academy Press
2101 Constitution Ave., NW
Box 285
Washington, DC 20055

800-624-6242
202-334-3313 (in the Washington metropolitan area)
http://www.nap.edu

Printed in the United States of America

THE NATIONAL ACADEMIES

National Academy of Sciences
National Academy of Engineering
Institute of Medicine
National Research Council

The **National Academy of Sciences** is a private, nonprofit, self-perpetuating society of distinguished scholars engaged in scientific and engineering research, dedicated to the furtherance of science and technology and to their use for the general welfare. Upon the authority of the charter granted to it by the Congress in 1863, the Academy has a mandate that requires it to advise the federal government on scientific and technical matters. Dr. Bruce M. Alberts is president of the National Academy of Sciences.

The **National Academy of Engineering** was established in 1964, under the charter of the National Academy of Sciences, as a parallel organization of outstanding engineers. It is autonomous in its administration and in the selection of its members, sharing with the National Academy of Sciences the responsibility for advising the federal government. The National Academy of Engineering also sponsors engineering programs aimed at meeting national needs, encourages education and research, and recognizes the superior achievements of engineers. Dr. William A. Wulf is president of the National Academy of Engineering.

The **Institute of Medicine** was established in 1970 by the National Academy of Sciences to secure the services of eminent members of appropriate professions in the examination of policy matters pertaining to the health of the public. The Institute acts under the responsibility given to the National Academy of Sciences by its congressional charter to be an adviser to the federal government and, upon its own initiative, to identify issues of medical care, research, and education. Dr. Kenneth I. Shine is president of the Institute of Medicine.

The **National Research Council** was organized by the National Academy of Sciences in 1916 to associate the broad community of science and technology with the Academy's purposes of furthering knowledge and advising the federal government. Functioning in accordance with general policies determined by the Academy, the Council has become the principal operating agency of both the National Academy of Sciences and the National Academy of Engineering in providing services to the government, the public, and the scientific and engineering communities. The Council is administered jointly by both Academies and the Institute of Medicine. Dr. Bruce M. Alberts and Dr. William A. Wulf are chairman and vice chairman, respectively, of the National Research Council.

COMMITTEE ON RESEARCH AND PEER REVIEW IN EPA

PAUL G. RISSER (*Chair*), Oregon State University, Corvallis
JULIAN B. ANDELMAN, University of Pittsburgh, Pittsburgh
ANDERS W. ANDREN, Univeristy of Wisconsin, Madison
JOHN C. BAILAR III, University of Chicago, Chicago
EULA BINGHAM, University of Cincinnati Medical Center, Cincinnati
DAVID S. C. CHU, RAND, Washington, D.C.
WALTER F. DABBERDT, National Center for Atmospheric Research, Boulder, Colo.
ROLF HARTUNG, University of Michigan, Ann Arbor
MORTON LIPPMANN, New York University Medical School, Tuxedo
RAYMOND C. LOEHR, University of Texas, Austin
JUDITH MCDOWELL, Woods Hole Oceanographic Institute, Woods Hole, Mass.
DAVID L. MORRISON, North Carolina State University, Raleigh
GEOFFREY PLACE, (retired: formerly Procter & Gamble), Hilton Head, S.C.
BAILUS WALKER, JR., Howard University College of Medicine, Washington, D.C.

Project Staff

JAMES J. REISA, Principal Staff Officer
RUTH E. CROSSGROVE, Editor
JAMIE YOUNG, Research Associate
MILLICENT ANDERSON, Assistant to the Director
PAMELA FRIEDMAN, Program Assistant

v

Preface

IN the three decades since the U.S. Environmental Protection Agency (EPA) was created, the agency's scientific and technical practices and credibility have been independently assessed many times in reports from the National Research Council (NRC), EPA Science Advisory Board, General Accounting Office, and many other organizations; in congressional oversight and judicial proceedings; and in countless criticisms and lawsuits from stakeholders with interests in particular EPA regulatory decisions. As a previous independent panel put it in the 1992 report *Safeguarding the Future: Credible Science, Credible Decisions*, EPA's policy and regulatory work receives a great deal of public attention, but the agency's scientific performance typically receives a similar degree of attention only when the scientific basis for a decision is questioned. Thus, strong scientific performance is important not only to enable EPA to make informed and effective decisions, but also to gain credibility and public support for the environmental protection efforts of EPA and the nation.

This report is the fourth and final one in a series prepared by two independent expert committees convened by the NRC in response to a request from Congress and to subsequent, related requests from EPA. The Committee on Research Opportunities and Priorities for EPA — our companion committee in this study — was charged to provide an overview of significant emerging environmental issues, identify and prioritize research themes most relevant to understanding and resolving

xi

those issues, and consider the role of EPA's research program in the context of research being conducted or supported by other organizations. That committee published an interim report in 1996 and a final report, *Building a Foundation for Sound Environmental Decisions*, in 1997. The Committee on Research and Peer Review in EPA—our committee—was charged to evaluate research management and scientific peer-review practices in the agency. Our committee published an interim report in 1995 and this final report. Specifically, our committee was given the following task:

> *The committee will perform an independent assessment of the U.S. Environmental Protection Agency's overall research and development program structure, peer review procedures, long-term research program, laboratory site review procedures, and research staff career development and performance evaluation procedures. In carrying out its charge, the committee will consider the mission-related research, development, and technical support needs of EPA's regulatory programs and regional offices; the role of EPA's research program in the context of research being conducted or sponsored by other agencies and organizations; and the problems and recommendations described in previous studies of these topics by the National Research Council, Carnegie Commission, and EPA Science Advisory Board.*

This report has been reviewed in draft form by individuals chosen for their technical expertise and diverse perspectives in accordance with procedures approved by the NRC's Report Review Committee for reviewing NRC and Institute of Medicine reports. The purpose of that independent review was to provide candid and critical comments to assist the NRC in making the published report as sound as possible and to ensure that the report meets institutional standards for objectivity, evidence, and responsiveness to the study charge. The review comments and draft manuscript remain confidential to protect the integrity of the deliberative process. We wish to thank the following individuals, who are neither officials nor employees of the NRC, for their participation in the review of this report: John Ahearne, Sigma Xi; James Anderson, Harvard University; Barry Bozeman, Georgia Institute of Technology; Richard Conway, (Retired, Union Carbide Corporation); Costel D. Denson, University of Delaware; Freeman Gilbert, University of California, San Diego; Gilbert Omenn, University of Michigan; William Raub, U.S. Department of Health and Human Services; W. Randall Seeker, Energy and Environmental Research Corporation; and Terry Yosie, Chemical Manufacturers Association.

The individuals listed above have provided many constructive comments and suggestions. It must be emphasized, however, that responsibility for the final content of this report rests entirely with the authoring committee and the NRC.

We gratefully acknowledge the contributions of more than 200 individuals from EPA and other agencies and organizations who made presentations, provided information, or otherwise aided the committee during the course of the study. We especially wish to thank Joseph Alexander, Robert Huggett, Henry Longest, Lisa Matthews, Norine Noonan, and Peter Preuss of EPA; Judy Bean, University of Miami; Ralph Cicerone, University of California at Irvine; Ellis Cowling, North Carolina State University; and Alan Krupnick, Resources for the Future.

We appreciate the assistance of the NRC staff in preparing the report. Staff members who contributed to this effort are James Reisa, director of the Board on Environmental Studies and Toxicology, who served as the NRC's principal staff officer; Jamie Young, research associate; Ruth Crossgrove, editor; Millicent Anderson, assistant to the director; Tracy Holby, senior program assistant; Pamela Friedman, project assistant; and Mirsada Karalic-Loncarevic, information specialist.

I would like to thank all my colleagues on the committee for their thoughtful contributions and dedicated efforts throughout the development of this report.

Finally, the members and staff of our committee wish to dedicate this report to the memory of Professor Donald W. Pritchard, a committee member who passed away last year. A renowned oceanographer and educator, Don had a distinguished academic career at the Johns Hopkins University, where he served as chairman of the department of oceanography and founded the Chesapeake Bay Institute, and at the State University of New York at Stony Brook, where he served as director of the Marine Science Research Center. Don's many honors included election to the National Academy of Engineering in 1993. We shall long remember the vast knowledge and wise counsel of this distinguished scholar.

Paul G. Risser
Chair, Committee on Research
and Peer Review in EPA

Contents

Strengthening Science at the U.S. Environmental Protection Agency:

Research-Management and Peer-Review Practices

Executive Summary

THE current strategic plan of the U.S. Environmental Protection Agency (EPA), published in 1997 in response to the Government Performance and Results Act, states that the agency's overall mission is to protect human health and to safeguard the natural environment. Charged to implement a disparate collection of federal laws that address various categories of environmental problems, EPA has been primarily a regulatory agency. It has not had a primary "science" mission in the same sense that the National Institutes of Health (NIH) or the National Science Foundation (NSF) have primary missions to advance scientific and technical knowledge through research. Yet, EPA's strategic plan strongly acknowledges that environmental protection efforts need to be "based on the best available scientific information," and "sound science" is one of the agency's avowed major goals.

Over the 3 decades since EPA was created, great progress has been achieved in cleaning up the nation's worst and most obvious environmental pollution problems, but many complex and difficult tasks remain. The environmental problems of today are often difficult to diagnose and treat; they cross state and national boundaries, entail difficult trade-offs, and sporadically present unpleasant surprises. Past illusions about simple and easy solutions to environmental problems have been replaced by the realization that environmental protection is often complicated and challenging.

1

Scientific knowledge and technical information are essential for determining which environmental problems pose important risks to human health, ecosystems, the quality of life, and the economy. We need scientific information to avoid wastefully targeting inconsequential problems while ignoring greater risks. We need such information to reduce uncertainties in environmental decision-making and to help develop cost-effective strategies to reduce risks. We need science to help identify emerging and future environmental problems and to prepare for the inevitable surprises.

This report is the fourth and final one in a series prepared by two companion expert committees convened by the National Research Council (NRC) in response to a request from Congress and to subsequent, related requests from EPA for an independent assessment of the overall structure and management of the agency's research program, as well as for an evaluation of scientific peer-review procedures used by EPA. To carry out the study, the NRC appointed the Committee on Research and Peer Review in EPA, which prepared an interim report addressing the initial request from Congress, and this, the final report in the study. Also as part of the study, the NRC appointed the Committee on Research Opportunities and Priorities for EPA, which prepared an interim report and the 1997 report *Building a Foundation for Sound Environmental Decisions*. This final report expands on issues discussed in the previous reports and addresses related questions.

The members of both committees are experts from the academic community and other organizations chosen by the NRC for their expertise in relevant scientific and technical disciplines. Special emphasis was placed on selecting committee members with research management experience and knowledge of the research and other scientific activities of EPA and other agencies. The chairman and two other members of the Committee on Research Opportunities and Priorities for EPA were also members of the Committee on Research and Peer Review in EPA.

In developing this report, the Committee on Research and Peer Review in EPA drew on the expertise and experience of its members and considered more than 300 relevant documents obtained from EPA and other sources. The committee consulted with more than 200 scientists, engineers, managers, and other persons within and outside EPA to obtain relevant information and insights on research-program structure, planning, funding, and management; organizational matters; and scientific career development, performance evaluation, recruitment, and morale issues. The committee held seven 2-day plenary meetings, six at facilities of the National Academies and one at the EPA laboratory facilities in Research Triangle Park, NC. In addition, smaller teams of committee members and staff made site visits to 12 EPA laboratory facilities across the country, in addition to all EPA regulatory offices and 5 of EPA's 10 regional offices. At these locations, committee members and staff interviewed a cross section of EPA personnel, including senior officials, middle managers, staff scientists and engineers, and support staff. During the course of the study, the committee also interviewed officials knowledgeable about EPA from Congress, the General Accounting Office (GAO), NSF, NIH, the Office of Management and Budget (OMB), and the Office of Science and Technology Policy (OSTP). In addition, most members of our committee have previously served on one or more groups that independently evaluated the research programs and scientific practices of EPA and other federal agencies under the auspices of the NRC, the Carnegie Commission, EPA's Scientific Advisory Board (SAB), the Office of Research and Development (ORD) Board of Scientific Counselors (BOSC), or other organizations. Such previous evaluations are cited and reviewed throughout our report.

On the basis of those documents, interviews, site visits, and previous experience with scientific practices in EPA, the committee recommends the following measures to strengthen the scientific performance of ORD and the agency overall.

SCIENTIFIC LEADERSHIP AND TALENT

Establish a new position at EPA: Deputy administrator for science and technology.

In the 30 years since EPA was created, the agency's scientific practices and performance have been criticized many times in reports from the NRC, EPA's SAB, the General Accounting Office, and many other organizations; in congressional oversight and judicial proceedings; and in countless criticisms and lawsuits from stakeholders with interests in particular EPA regulatory decisions. In one such report, *Safeguarding the Future: Credible Science, Credible Decisions,* a panel of academicians, including two members of our committee, concluded, "Currently, EPA science is of uneven quality, and the Agency's policies and regulations are frequently perceived as lacking a strong scientific foundation." While acknowledging that EPA had a number of knowledgeable scientists on its staff, the panel reported that the science base at EPA was not *perceived* to be strong by the university community, and that many EPA scientists at all levels throughout the agency believed that EPA did not use their scientific knowledge and resources effectively. The panel further observed, "A perception exists that regulations based on unsound science have led to unneeded economic and social burdens, and that unsound science has sometimes led to decisions that expose people and ecosystems to avoidable risks." The panel commented that EPA had not always ensured that contrasting, reputable scientific views were well-explored and well-documented from the beginning to the end of the regulatory process. It pointed out that the agency was often perceived to have a conflict of interest because it needed science to support its regulatory activities, and it described a widely held perception by people both outside and inside the agency, that EPA science was "adjusted" by EPA scientists or decision-makers, consciously or unconsciously, to fit policy.

As discussed in many places throughout this report, EPA has made significant improvements in some of its scientific practices since that panel issued its report in 1992. However, the committee concludes that there is a continuing basis for many of the scientific concerns raised in that panel's report and others, such as the 1999 Resources for the Future report *Science at EPA: Information in the Regulatory Process.* We base this conclusion on the extensive experience of the members of our committee in assessing EPA's scientific practices and performance, including the matters discussed and documents cited in this report and other independent investigations of EPA science in which members of our committee have participated.

Throughout EPA's history, no official below the level of the administrator has had overall responsibility or authority for the scientific and technical foundations of agency decisions, and administrators of EPA have typically been trained in law, not science. The agency's most senior science official has traditionally been the assistant administrator for research and development, but that official has never had agency-wide responsibility or authority for overseeing the scientific and technical basis for regulatory and policy decision-making, and EPA's regulatory offices are not required to follow scientific advice from ORD. In the committee's unanimous judgment, the lack of a top science official is a formula for weak scientific performance in the agency and poor scientific credibility outside the agency.   In our 1995 interim report, this committee recommended "that the assistant administrator for research and development be designated as EPA's chief scientific and technical officer, responsible not only for ORD, but also for coordinating and overseeing agency-wide scientific policy, peer review, and quality assurance, as well as EPA's outreach to the broader domestic and international scientific community for scientific knowledge relevant to the agency's mission." Shortly thereafter, in partial response to that recommendation, the deputy administrator of EPA asked the head of ORD to coordinate the agency's scientific-planning and peer-review activities.

Although the 1995 designation appears to have been a small step in the right direction, our committee judges it to be insufficient. First, the head of ORD was not given real authority for agency-wide scientific policy. Second, although the agency subsequently achieved some commendable progress through its interoffice Science Policy Council and ORD-led efforts to begin developing an agency-wide inventory of scientific activities and a "Strategic Framework for EPA Science," all those efforts, relying on consensus and voluntary cooperation of the agency's regulatory and regional offices in the absence of central science-policy authority, have had slow and limited success.   The heads of EPA's regulatory and regional offices are of equal rank to the head of ORD and are generally not required to follow ORD's guidance regarding scientific activities or science policy. Third, the ability of the head of ORD to coordinate agency-wide peer-review and quality-assurance practices was diminished in 1999 with the reassignment of some peer-review functions from ORD to the agency's newly created Office of Environmental Information.

Furthermore, based on our observations of these developments in the 5 years since our interim report, the committee has become convinced that our 1995 recommendation to designate the head of ORD as

EPA's chief scientific and technical officer also was insufficient. The committee now concludes that it underestimated in 1995 the level of authority needed to achieve the necessary degree of cooperation and coordination of scientific activities and policy in the regulatory and regional offices. In addition, the committee has become more aware of the enormous amount of scientific activity occurring in EPA's regulatory and regional offices, and it concludes that no single individual could reasonably be expected to direct a world-class research program in ORD while also trying to improve scientific practices and performance throughout the rest of the agency. These jobs are inherently different. Moreover, assigning agency-wide scientific authority to the assistant administrator for ORD might produce a conflict of responsibilities, because many decisions about science in the regulatory programs could affect ORD's budget or favor ORD's research over research done elsewhere.

EPA needs an appropriately qualified science official at a sufficiently high level to carry both the authority and the responsibility for agency-wide scientific performance. No official below the level of deputy administrator could perform that role, because interrelated scientific and technical activities are conducted throughout the agency. The requisite operating authority with accountability for agency-wide scientific performance cannot be established by assigning the scientific gate-keeper function to any assistant administrator, regardless of the qualifications or abilities of the individual holding that position. It is unrealistic to expect that an official at the level of an assistant administrator (i.e., an official in charge of one office of EPA) could effectively coordinate and oversee the scientific and technical programs and work products of other EPA offices and regions. That includes the assistant administrator in charge of ORD.

EPA needs a top science official with the authority and responsibility to coordinate and oversee scientific activities throughout the agency. This official should obtain and use the best possible science in support of the agency's mission and identify the scientific uncertainties and conflicting evidence relevant to the agency's regulatory and policy decisions. The importance of science in EPA decision-making should be no less than that afforded to legal considerations. Just as the advice of the agency's general counsel is relied upon by the administrator to determine whether a proposed action is "legal," an appropriately qualified and adequately empowered science official is needed to attest to the administrator and the nation that the proposed action is "scientific" — that it is consistent, or at least not inconsistent, with available scientific knowledge — and that the agency has done a proper job of ascertaining and applying that knowledge and recognizing and characterizing the relevant uncertainties. Achieving these goals will require a level of accountability for EPA's scientific performance that cannot reasonably be expected from an administrator who is not trained in science, a staff advisor to the administrator without management authority, or an assistant administrator for research and development who has no authority over the use of scientific information by other offices of the agency.

The creation of a new position of deputy administrator for science and technology will require authorization from Congress, appointment by the President, and confirmation by the Senate. Such an action would send a strong message that Congress and the administration are committed to strengthening science at EPA. The current position of deputy administrator could perhaps become deputy administrator for policy and management.

The new deputy administrator for science and technology would be responsible for identifying and defining the important scientific issues facing EPA, including those embedded in major policy or regulatory proposals; developing and overseeing an integrated agency-wide strategy for acquiring, disseminating, and applying scientific information; coordinating and overseeing scientific quality-assurance and peer-review practices throughout the agency; developing processes to ensure that appropriate scientific information is used in decision-making throughout the agency, and ensuring that the scientific and technical information underlying each EPA regulatory decision is valid, appropriately characterized in terms of scientific uncertainty and cross-media issues, and appropriately applied.

The deputy administrator for science and technology would be the administrator's principal science advisor and would have managerial authority to coordinate and oversee the agency's ORD, the newly created Office of Environmental Information, the SAB, the Science Policy Council, and the scientific and technical activities of the agency's regulatory program and regional offices. The individual appointed to this position would need to have an outstanding background, including research accomplishments, scientific reputation, and experience in public forums.

Convert the position of assistant administrator for research and development to a statutory term appointment of 6 years.

Under the present political-appointment model, the leadership of ORD changes at least as often as the administration changes. Historically, the typical tenure of ORD assistant administrators has been only about 2 or 3 years. Frequent changes in the leadership of ORD have been disruptive and have had devastating effects on the continuity of programs, and sometimes on the morale of ORD scientists and staff. Over the years, the assistant administrator for ORD has typically been one of the last senior EPA officers appointed in a new administration, and although ORD has had some very capable assistant administrators, there have been a few cases in which little weight seems to have been given to the candidate's scientific or managerial qualifications.

The assistant administrator for ORD should have an advanced degree in an appropriate scientific or technological discipline, a substantial record of scholarly achievement, and administrative experience that includes successful management of a substantial research program. The position should be defined to make it attractive to an eminent scientist or engineer who is willing to remain in the position for a sufficiently long period of time to bring stability to the direction and leadership of ORD. A statutory term appointment would make the position more like those of the leaders of NIH or NSF. Congressional action would be required to convert the position to the recommended 6-year term.

Seek ways to give research managers in ORD a high degree of flexibility and commensurate accountability. Empower and charge them to make research program decisions at the lowest appropriate management level consistent with EPA policy and ORD's strategic goals and budget priorities.

Excellence at EPA, or elsewhere, requires effective leadership at many levels, not just at the top. In the selection and advancement of managers at all levels in ORD laboratories and centers, competence in management and supervision should be emphasized, but scientific and technical qualifications and accomplishments should also be given strong consideration. Research managers should understand the work and merit the respect of their research staff while having the ability to select, inspire, lead, and elicit the best efforts from other scientists and engineers. They should be strong advocates and defenders of the continuity and core capabilities required for the conduct of a good research program. EPA's ability to recruit, develop, and retain such leaders depends on many factors, including the agency's commitment to reducing bureaucratic impediments and finding ways to increase the latitude afforded to research managers to fulfill their responsibilities.

Enhance research leadership and ORD's scientific stature by creating the equivalent of endowed academic research chairs in ORD's national laboratories.

In research, perhaps even more than in other fields, pre-eminent leadership sets the standard and tone for the rest of the work force. A single world-class investigator can generate ideas and enthusiasm to elevate a research program dramatically. In research, leadership is not synonymous with management or administration.

The 1992 *Safeguarding the Future* report recommended that ORD recruit and support on a long-term basis four to six senior research scientists and engineers with world-class reputations in areas vital to EPA's long-term strategy and direction. The panel envisioned that these eminent scientists and engineers would serve as examples and mentors for all scientists in EPA and would bring access to networks of world-class scientists to benefit the agency. The panel recommended that EPA's SAB be asked to form a search committee.

ORD responded to the 1992 recommendation by obtaining and using special authority to recruit and promote research scientists and engineers to senior, nonmanagerial federal career positions—so-called ST (scientific and technical) positions at the Senior Executive Service level. Using merit-review panels that included outside experts to evaluate candidates, ORD has recruited or promoted eight such individuals in its laboratories. Our committee fully supports ORD's use of the ST program and urges that it be continued. However, recognizing today's intense job-market competition with industry and academic institutions for top research talent, the committee concludes that even greater measures are warranted and practicable to attract and retain outstanding research leaders in the ORD laboratories.

To establish the recommended "research chair" positions, ORD could explore the possibility of awarding prestigious 5-year renewable grants or distinguished fellowships to distinguished academic scientists to work at ORD laboratories on site, full time. The committee suggests that it is not necessary for all such researchers to be regular federal employees. Alternatively, ORD could seek authority to create and fill positions similar to NIH Title 42 senior research appointments, perhaps in connection with internal grants to ensure sustained research support for these distinguished investigators. The SAB or the BOSC should be asked to assist ORD in developing this program and selecting the candidates.

Our committee envisions the recruitment of at least one additional distinguished investigator per ORD national laboratory in areas of research that are rapidly advancing and important to ORD's future. These individuals should be given maximum intellectual freedom to pursue productive lines of research that are consistent with laboratory missions and ORD priorities. The distinguished investigators should be expected to serve as mentors and role models for other ORD research scientists but should have no managerial responsibility beyond their own on-site research teams.

Continue to place high priority on the ORD graduate fellowship and postdoctoral programs.

To achieve scientific and technical excellence, EPA must attract, retain, and properly support a first-rate, dedicated professional staff. Our committee is aware of many outstanding scientists and engineers in ORD and other parts of the agency, but the ORD work force is aging. More than 47% of ORD's employees are at least 50 years old, and more than 550 ORD employees will be eligible to retire within the next 5 years. Periodic EPA hiring freezes, combined with intense scientific and technical job-market competition from the private sector and academic institutions, have made it extremely difficult for ORD to recruit the new talent needed to sustain and enhance its research work force or even to retain some of the best of those on board.

Since 1995, ORD has established excellent programs of graduate fellowships and postdoctoral appointments. These programs have brought a stream of fresh scientific and technical talent into EPA's research program and are helping to train future research leaders in environmental science, engineering, and other disciplines. The committee urges EPA to continue to place high priority on these programs.

RESEARCH CONTINUITY AND BALANCE

Continue steadily on the major courses set in the 1995 reorganization of ORD.

EPA's ORD conducts research in its in-house laboratories, funds extramural research at academic institutions and other organizations, performs a variety of activities in the development and application of risk-assessment methods and regulatory criteria, and provides technical services in support of the mission of the agency and its regulatory and regional offices. In fiscal year 1999, ORD had 1,976 staff members at 12 geographically dispersed laboratory facilities, three field stations, three assessment offices, and the headquarters office in Washington, DC. ORD also had an extramural research budget of about $315 million—more than half of its $559 million total budget in fiscal year 1999—for grants, cooperative and interagency agreements, contracts, and fellowships. Over the past 20 years, the resources of ORD generally comprised about 7% of the agency's total budget.

Frequent changes in goals, priorities, practices, structure, or funding can disrupt any organization, but they are especially damaging to a research organization, which has special requirements for continuity in the development and maintenance of scientific and engineering talent, experience, and infrastructure to be productive. Maintaining the requisite degree of stability in ORD has been a continuing challenge because of many expansions and other changes in EPA's legislative mandates and priorities, directives from Congress and different administrations, pressures from regulated parties and other interest groups, lawsuits and court decisions, inadequate budgets to meet competing demands, and changes in the leadership of ORD.

ORD has changed its research goals, priorities, and practices often and abruptly in the past. Greater stability, continuity, and predictability are among the most important needs in the ORD program. The limited financial and human resources of ORD should be managed with a steady hand and a clear and persistent vision of how to maximize the gains in scientific understanding resulting from its work.

Our committee's interim report endorsed the general scope and direction of the major reorganization of ORD in 1995, which adopted as a principal organizing concept the reduction of uncertainty in risk assessment and risk management, initiated a new strategic research planning process, consolidated ORD's laboratories and centers, and expanded and strengthened the research grants, centers, fellowships, and peer-review programs. Our interim report called those measures the most important changes in the history of EPA's research program. In the long run, the courses ORD set in 1995 should have a stabilizing effect on the research program, and our committee continues to support them. In some respects those changes are still a work in progress and need more time to mature.

Continue and expand ORD's new multiyear planning approaches for both problem-driven and core research areas.

In the past few years, ORD has begun to explore a multiyear approach for research planning to foster continuity and strategic integration of some research efforts. ORD has developed multiyear plans for research on particulate matter, endocrine disruptors, drinking water, environmental monitoring, global climate change, and pollution prevention. Multiyear plans for additional areas of research are under development. The plans are developed by research teams from ORD laboratories and centers and are peer reviewed. Our committee expects that ORD's recent efforts in multiyear planning will contribute to research program continuity and the achievement of strategic goals, and the committee commends ORD for these initiatives.

Maintain approximately an even balance between problem-driven research and core research.

ORD is challenged to lead the agency by means of research while continuing to assist its client regulators, some of whom have limited understanding or appreciation of science but a strong say in ORD's budget and priorities. Activities in support of regulatory programs often have a narrow focus and often compete to pre-empt long-term research programs. They tend to be disruptive and to consume the resources of a research organization disproportionately. Regulatory strategies, which are typically prescriptive and specific, tend to freeze concepts and methods in time, and the more closely that ORD is tied to the regulatory programs, the greater the risk that ORD will to some extent be working on outdated problems or with outdated approaches.

On the other hand, ORD's involvement in problem-driven research and technical assistance to regulatory and regional offices has important benefits for ORD's own core research as well as for the agency's operating programs. Perhaps the greatest dividends are the resulting improvements in the scientific aspects of the agency's regulatory actions and the maintenance of an in-house scientific core group experienced in dealing with environmental risks and programs. An experienced scientific core group can be of great value in meeting emergency requirements for technical expertise. ORD's technical assistance provides the regulatory offices with competent scientific help and leadership, and it enables ORD's research scientists to keep abreast of regulatory and policy developments elsewhere in EPA.

In the 1997 NRC report *Building a Foundation for Sound Environmental Decisions*, our companion committee in this study concluded that ORD should maintain a balance between the problem-driven research and technical support for the agency's regulatory programs and the core research to better understand and anticipate environmental risks. Our committee agrees. Those two functions are not unrelated or incompatible; they are mutually reinforcing. Core research is the indispensable wellspring that prepares and enables ORD to provide better problem-specific research and technical assistance to the agency and the nation.

RESEARCH PARTNERSHIPS AND OUTREACH

Develop and implement a pro-active, structured, and visible strategy for stimulating, acquiring, and applying the results of research conducted or sponsored by other federal and state agencies, universities, and industry in this country and abroad.

From time to time the question arises whether EPA should have its own research program or rely on research results developed elsewhere.

Advocates of having the research conducted elsewhere often cite past criticisms of the agency's research program and point to excellent research programs of other agencies, such as NIH, NSF, and the Department of Energy, that collectively, and in some cases individually, dwarf that of EPA. And, of course, the academic community and the private sector conduct much of the research relevant to EPA's mission.

In the 1992 report *Safeguarding the Future: Credible Science, Credible Decisions*, a panel of four senior academicians, including two members of our committee, concluded that EPA needs its own strong science base to provide the background required for effective environmental protection programs. Similarly, *Building a Foundation for Sound Environmental Decisions*, the 1997 report of the NRC's Committee on Research Opportunities and Priorities for EPA—our companion committee in this study—concluded that EPA needs a strong in-house research program.

Our committee agrees that a vigorous research program should be maintained in EPA. Moving the research program out of the agency would most likely weaken, not strengthen, the scientific foundation of EPA's decisions and actions. Although some abstract concept of scientific "quality" might be improved by reducing some kinds of ORD technical work that are unlikely to advance research frontiers, such work is often critically necessary to EPA's pursuit of its mission and statutory responsibilities. Overall, eliminating ORD or moving its functions out of EPA would be destructive, and the level of damage would increase with passing time as EPA became increasingly unable to pursue, apply, or even understand new research knowledge. An EPA devoid of a research program would not be likely to attract substantial scientific talent, and an EPA without scientific talent would be ineffective and potentially harmful to the nation.

However, even with a much larger budget, ORD could never meet all the vast and constantly expanding needs of EPA and the nation for scientific and technical knowledge to guide environmental protection efforts. ORD has had a first-rate research program in some important areas, such as aquatic toxicology and human inhalation toxicology, but it is not possible for ORD to be a leader across the full range of scientific knowledge required by EPA. The agency should recognize the limits of its research capabilities and develop an effective, structured, and visible strategy to acquire, use, and support research in areas where ORD cannot be pre-eminent. The strategy should include a program of increased sabbatical assignments for ORD researchers to gain experience in other scientific organizations, and more visiting appointments of scientists and engineers from universities, other government agencies, and private organizations to work in ORD laboratories and centers.

Reassess the numbers, qualifications, and skill mix of the staff of ORD's National Center for Environmental Research to ensure they are consistent with the needs of the current program of research grants, centers, and fellowships.

ORD's expanded and strengthened competitive research grants, centers, and fellowships programs have greatly increased the number and activities of talented academic researchers across the nation who are engaged in research relevant to EPA's mission. ORD deserves to be commended for its excellent performance in developing and implementing these programs, as well as for the partnerships it has built with other agencies and funding organizations in joint grant solicitations. However, as discussed in Chapter 2, questions have been raised about the adequacy of the numbers, qualifications, and skill mix of the staff of ORD's National Center for Environmental Research to administer the grants, centers, and fellowships programs. Since 1995, ORD has increased the research-grant funds administered by the center by about 400% without substantially increasing the staff who administer this program. The increased grant-program activity has placed high demands on the staff who are responsible for the review process and the monitoring and dissemination of grantees' research products. And the staff who administer EPA's Science to Achieve Results (STAR) program grants must address mission-relevance and technology-transfer aspects of grantee's research that NIH and NSF grants administrators are not required to address.

Develop additional mechanisms to promote and facilitate research interactions among STAR grantees and ORD research staff.

The committee encourages strengthening the interactions between STAR grantees and research scientists and engineers in the ORD laboratories. At present, there are insufficient mechanisms for facilitating such interactions effectively. One possible mechanism is to ask grant applicants to identify in their proposals how their research might be enhanced by interactions with EPA scientists and how their research might complement or supplement ongoing or planned research in the ORD laboratories. Reviewers of the proposals, as well as ORD scientists and the SAB, could also be asked for suggestions.

Increase EPA's efforts to disseminate actively ORD's research products, to explain their significance, and to assist others inside and outside the agency in applying them.

The 1992 *Safeguarding the Future* report concluded that the academic community, Congress, other federal agencies, industry, the public, and even many within EPA are generally unfamiliar with the work of EPA scientists. The 1992 panel emphasized that many officials involved in funding EPA science were uncertain about what science products EPA had produced, and whether the quality and quantity of its products were commensurate with the dollars expended. It noted that EPA's policy and regulatory work receives a great deal of public attention, but the agency's science typically receives a similar degree of attention only when the scientific basis for a decision is questioned. The panel concluded that EPA should strive to make more widely known the short-term and long-term scientific goals and achievements of its research laboratories, contractors, and grantees. It urged the agency to develop and implement a coherent communications, outreach, and education plan to publicize the activities and accomplishments of EPA scientists.

Even within the agency, many regulatory and regional program officials throughout EPA's history have been largely unaware and even dubious of any important benefits from ORD's research program, and consequently they have not been supportive of ORD's budget. Recently, the GAO reported that one of EPA's regulatory program offices so acutely needed information on ORD's work—information relevant to its program and well beyond the progress reports that ORD was providing—that the regulatory office found it necessary to pay for the development of a system to track ORD's projects. That kind of situation is not healthful for ORD or the agency. ORD's ongoing efforts to disseminate its research products and inform others about them have, with some exceptions, been meager and unimaginative.

Publication of original research articles is critically important, but it is not sufficient. EPA should publish more individual research-topic-area summaries and comprehensive annual summaries of the results of in-house and extramural research and technical-support activities. The summaries should be planned and tailored for specific audiences and should emphasize the potential applications of ORD's work by other EPA offices, state agencies, industry, and others.

In addition, our committee concurs with the 1998 recommendation of ORD's BOSC that the National Center for Environmental Assessment should revise its mission to focus more on being an advisor, catalyst, and resource for the risk assessments performed by the rest of the agency, rather than trying itself to do individual risk assessments with its own limited resources. The center should focus on being a research organization dedicated to advancing the state of practice in risk assessment. It should reduce its role as a performer of individual risk assessments that could be done by EPA's regulatory offices.

RESEARCH ACCOUNTABILITY

Improve the documentation and transparency of the decision-making processes used by ORD for setting research and technical-assistance priorities, making intramural and extramural assignments, and allocating funds.

In commenting on ORD's fiscal year 2000 budget, the SAB indicated that the lack of transparency in the decision-making process used by ORD to set research priorities made it difficult to evaluate the adequacy of the proposed budget. Although the ORD strategic plan discusses the general processes and criteria by which decisions are made on research priorities and funding allocations, the plan describes the processes and criteria only in very broad terms.

During the committee's site visits and interviews, the staff of some EPA regulatory program offices expressed the belief that they have little influence on ORD's research priorities through the Research Coordination Council or any other mechanism. They felt that they needed a stronger voice in the setting of ORD's priorities, and that ORD should be held more accountable to the agency's other offices for performing agreed-upon tasks.

Our committee concludes that ORD should continue to be responsive to the agency's regulatory offices for the problem-driven and technical-assistance components of its program, and the agency's regulatory offices should continue to have a strong voice in decisions about the ORD plans and budget elements devoted to those components. For the core-research portion of its program, however, ORD should have greater freedom to set the agenda, without the need for specific concurrence of regulatory program offices that are focused on statutory requirements and regulatory goals. In the agency planning process, ORD should continue to consider the views and needs of the program offices in developing both components of its program, but it should maintain an adequate degree of independence in planning a core-research program that will successfully perform the leadership and anticipatory-research role that such a program can bring to the agency.

The process by which ORD decides whether a project or task is to be performed by in-house staff or through one or more extramural mechanisms is also of crucial importance to the quality of the work and the cost-effective management of resources. This decision-making process has not been sufficiently open or visible for persons outside ORD or EPA to reconstruct or assess how the decisions were made.

Expand upon the recently initiated agency-wide science inventory by conducting, documenting, and publishing a more comprehensive and detailed inventory of all scientific activities that are being conducted by offices throughout EPA.

ORD's research should not be the only scientific studies held accountable in EPA. A great deal of research-like activity, including many activities in scientific and technical data-gathering, analysis, and interpretation, are being conducted or funded by EPA offices outside ORD. Much of this work is not labeled "research." The other offices of EPA do not have the kind of authorization that ORD has to conduct research per se, and full disclosure might risk the loss of control of such activities by the regulatory offices. Historically, many of the scientific studies and analysis performed or funded outside ORD were not fully coordinated across the agency or included in the ORD's research-planning and peer-review programs. Our committee is by no means opposed to scientific studies and analyses being conducted in parts of the agency outside ORD, but such activities require transparency, quality assurance, and accountability, just as ORD's program does.

ORD, with the help of others throughout the agency, recently initiated an inventory of science projects and programs across EPA. Our committee commends the agency for this important step. We recommend that the administrator direct the new deputy administrator for science and technology to expand on the preliminary-inventory by documenting a more comprehensive and detailed inventory of scientific activities conducted by all EPA offices. The inventory should include information well beyond the current scope — information such as goals and objectives of each project, milestones, schedules, principal investigators and project managers, and allocations of staff and financial resources. The results of the inventory should be used to ensure that such activities are properly coordinated through the agency-wide science-planning and budgeting process and are appropriately peer reviewed. The SAB should be engaged in assisting and overseeing this effort.

SCIENTIFIC PEER REVIEW

Change the agency's peer-review policy to more strictly separate the management of the development of a work product from the management of the peer review of that work product, thereby ensuring greater independence of peer reviews from the control of program managers, or the potential appearance of control by program managers, throughout the agency.

The committee congratulates EPA and its Science Policy Council for the excellent progress it has made in strengthening and expanding the agency's peer-review practices. The agency's 1998 peer-review handbook, discussed in Chapter 3, is a valuable resource and guidance document.

EPA's SAB has expressed concern about potential conflict of interest on the part of peer-review leaders — individuals assigned to manage reviews of agency work products — because current agency policy allows the same individual to be a project manager for the development of a particular work product and the peer-review leader for the same work product. The SAB noted that such a manager might have a special interest in the outcome of the review and might therefore be unable to ensure the essential degree of independence. The SAB contrasted EPA's present policy with the agency's data-quality-assurance practices, whereby a staff officer is empowered to stop activity if there is a quality-assurance problem.

EPA has made excellent progress in expanding and strengthening its peer-review practices, but the agency should find a way to ensure a greater degree of independence in the management of its peer reviews. The committee acknowledges that the agency should have adequate flexibility to accommodate statutory and court deadlines and resource limitations. Nevertheless, independence is essential to the proper and credible functioning of the peer-review process, and EPA's current policies fail to ensure adequate independence. Our committee shares the SAB's concern about the potential for conflicts of interest of EPA peer-review leaders and decision-makers. Despite good intentions, and even if the current policy works well much of the time, some of these individuals, under pressure to meet a deadline or implement a regulatory policy, might be tempted to compromise the integrity of the peer-review process for some work products by making convenient or improper decisions on the form of peer review, the selection of reviewers, the specification of charges to the reviewers, or the responses to reviewers' comments.

Our committee believes that the decision-maker and peer-review leader for a work product should never be the same person, and that wherever practicable, the peer-review leader should not report to the same organizational unit as the decision-maker. The committee recognizes that statutory and judicial deadlines can make it necessary that a program-office decision-maker retains the authority to proceed with an action on a provisional basis in the face of concerns or objections from a peer-review leader, the final decision being made by the EPA administrator. However, the independent decisions and any objections of a peer-review leader should be preserved and made a part of the agency decision package and public record for a work product. If such an independent assessment produces criticism of the adequacy or outcome of a peer review, EPA's policy should be to ensure that the criticism is clearly noted and that the reasons for proceeding despite the criticism are clearly explained.

The committee also recommends that the Science Policy Council's reviews of the agency's peer-review handbook and of experiences with its implementation include an explicit focus on promoting appropriate forms and levels of review for different types of work products and on reducing unnecessarily complex or inefficient requirements. The Science Policy Council should not necessarily wait the 5-year interval specified in the peer-review handbook; it should make changes as needed. The agency cannot afford to allow unnecessary or inefficient requirements to continue so long. The Science Policy Council's review should be ongoing. We also recommend that the Science Policy Council review a true random sample of peer-reviewed work products, examining the decisions made in structuring the review, the responses to review, and the cost, quality, timeliness, and impact of the review.

Finally, the committee wishes to emphasize that peer review must become accepted throughout EPA as a part of the agency's culture—a tool for improving quality—not merely a bureaucratic requirement. Measures such as periodic dissemination of the impacts and benefits of completed reviews might help to foster this cultural change in the agency.

1

Evaluating Science at EPA

THE ROLE OF SCIENCE AT EPA

IN the three decades since the U.S. Environmental Protection Agency (EPA) was created, great progress has been achieved in cleaning up the nation's worst and most obvious environmental pollution problems. Belching smokestacks and raw-sewage discharges are now scarce, and air pollution alerts and beach closings are more rare. EPA deserves a significant share of the credit for the accomplishments, but some of the most difficult and challenging tasks remain. Many past illusions about simple and easy solutions to environmental problems have been replaced by greater realization that environmental protection is a complicated and challenging mission.

Today, scientific knowledge and technical information are more important than ever for understanding and successfully addressing the increasingly complex environmental problems facing the nation. In the 1970s, environmental protection efforts and the associated demands for scientific knowledge were largely and appropriately focused on the manufacturing and transportation sectors and the problems associated with environmental releases at the sources. Today, there is a greater recognition that this is a limited view of the environmental problems challenging public health and the environment. Such problems can arise from environmental releases during all stages of a product's life cycle, including manufacturing, distribution, use, and disposal. Further, the problems are not associated solely with the pollutants released directly, but are often the result of complex reactions and interactions occurring in the environment, such as those associated with the formation of ozone in the troposphere or the formation and bioaccumulation of methyl mercury. Such problems can only be addressed through an understanding of the complex interrelationships among environmental media (air, water, land, and biota), human health and ecology, and economic sectors.

Along with the growing need for scientific knowledge and technical information to understand these complex factors are the rapidly occurring scientific advances in fields as diverse as molecular biology, chemistry, medicine, information technology, and the social sciences. These advances and the knowledge and technology they create hold the key to our future ability to identify and understand the environmental problems that pose the greatest risks to human health, environmental quality, natural resources, the economy, and our quality of life. Such advances in scientific knowledge and technological capability are also critical in the development of strategies for reducing environmental risks. In addition, advances in the social and behavioral sciences, including qualitative-analysis, risk-communication, and stakeholder-engagement techniques, are increasingly recognized as critical components of risk-reduction strategies.

Scientific knowledge and technical information are also needed to set environmental priorities. In the absence of sound scientific information, high-risk problems might not be adequately addressed, while high-profile but lower-risk problems might be targeted wastefully. When scientific knowledge is unavailable or overlooked, regulations and policies may fail to address serious environmental problems or unnecessarily seek to overprotect every person or every ecosystem against hazards that are minor or that few will actually experience. This can carry serious implications for public health and the environment or impose a heavy burden on society and the economy without providing appreciably better protection for most people or ecosystems.

Scientific knowledge is also needed to help identify and prepare for emerging and future environmental problems, including problems not envisioned or addressed by current statutes and government programs. If scientists can identify emerging or future environmental trends and their consequences, early steps can be designed to avoid or reduce the risks posed by those trends, thereby avoiding the much larger costs of addressing problems after they have grown to serious proportions.

As stated in *Safeguarding the Future: Credible Science, Credible Decisions* (EPA 1992),

> [S]*cience is one of the soundest investments the nation can make for the future. Strong science provides the foundation for credible environmental decision making. With a better understanding of environmental risks to people and ecosystems, EPA can target the hazards that pose the greatest risks, anticipate environmental problems before they reach a critical level, and develop strategies that use the nation's, and the world's, environmental protection dollars wisely.*

EPA was created in 1970 by presidential executive order, not by legislation. Although a principal justification for creating the agency was the need for a unified environmental program for the nation (CEQ 1970), the programs and capabilities of EPA over the years have derived from a disparate collection of federal statutes that use varying approaches to address separate environmental problem areas but lack a unified approach to protect the environment and public health.

Although no formal overall mission has ever been enacted for EPA, the agency has published a strategic plan (EPA 1997b), developed in response to the 1993 Government Performance and Results Act. It states,

> *The mission of the U.S. Environmental Protection Agency is to protect human health and to safeguard the natural environment — air, water, and land — upon which life depends.*

Thus, EPA does not primarily have a "science" mission in the same sense that the National Institutes of Health (NIH) or the National Science Foundation (NSF) have primary missions to advance scientific and technical knowledge through research. Traditionally, EPA has mainly been a "command-and-control" regulatory agency. Alternatives to regulatory action in some areas have been explored, but the agency's first priority has been to implement and enforce the statutes, mostly regulatory, under which it operates. Science has been an important part of the basis for many agency decisions and actions, but it has not been the only basis, and in many cases it has not even been a major determinant of EPA's decisions. EPA's past decisions and actions have largely been driven by the requirements of regulatory statutes and the policies and priorities of each administration.

Nevertheless, EPA's strategic plan (EPA 1997b) states that one of the agency's seven overall purposes is to ensure that "National efforts to reduce environmental risk are based on the best available scientific information." In addition, one of the agency's 10 major goals, also stated in the strategic plan, is the following:

> *Sound Science, Improved Understanding of Environmental Risk, and Greater Innovation to Address Environmental Problems: EPA will develop and apply the best available science for addressing current and future environmental hazards, as well as new approaches toward improving environmental protection.*

EPA's strategic plan also states,

> *Science enables us to identify the most important sources of risk to human health and the environment, and by so doing, informs our priority-setting, ensures credibility for our policies, and guides our deployment of resources. It gives us the understanding and technologies we need to detect, abate, and avoid environmental problems. This goal recognizes that science provides the crucial underpinning for EPA decisions and challenges us to apply the best available science and technical analysis to our environmental problems and to practice more integrated, more efficient, and more effective approaches to reducing environmental risks.*

The agency promised (EPA 1997b) the following future scientific accomplishments over the next decade:

> *EPA's research program will measurably increase our understanding of environmental processes and our capability to respond to and solve environmental problems. During the past decade, significant concerns have been expressed about the adequacy of the Agency's ability to assess risks — not only to human health, but also to ecosystems. Research will*

lead to greater certainty in assessing and comparing environmental risks. Our aim is to reduce major areas of uncertainty in our analyses of risk and to minimize reliance on default assumptions. In order to accomplish this, we will develop improved exposure assessments that identify environmental exposures posing the greatest environmental risks to the American public and will increasingly use biologically-based methodologies. We will demonstrate improved knowledge of current ecosystem conditions and the most critical stressors affecting these conditions, as well as deliver improved capabilities to interpret what these conditions imply in terms of immediate and future risks. This will provide strengthened capability to determine the condition of the environment and its responses to alternative management strategies at local, regional, and national scales. This will also lead to better technologies to manage and restore ecosystems.

We will also build institutional capacity to forecast and prepare for emerging problems. To prevent damage to both human and ecosystem health, it is critical to detect, describe, evaluate, and mitigate or eliminate stressors before damage occurs. We plan to improve capacity and technology to monitor and model stressors and effects. We plan to encourage the rapid acceptance and implementation of improved environmental technology by assessing and verifying the performance characteristics of commercially ready technologies and by making those assessments available for consideration by a variety of potential technology users. This will help provide proven, cost-effective technologies and approaches to prevent or manage environmental problems.

The Agency plans to strengthen the science base of the Regions by increasing their capacity to monitor and measure environmental conditions. We also plan to strengthen our overall quality of science by significantly enhancing peer review in the Agency and by seeking guidance from the Science Advisory Board, leading to more defensible environmental decisions.

Since scientific quality and cost-effectiveness are generally increased through collegial interaction, the Agency plans to increase its "partnering" with other Agencies and organizations, especially in joint efforts through the National Science and Technology Council, and in more frequent collaboration with NASA, NSF, and DOE. Similar synergistic benefits are sought through joint participation in the peer review of Agency documents and positions by advisory committees from different departments and agencies.

The following report examines EPA practices and the likelihood of achieving these worthy goals.

PREVIOUS ASSESSMENTS OF SCIENCE AT EPA

In the 30 years since EPA was created, the agency's scientific performance has been assessed many times in reports from the National Research Council (NRC), the EPA Science Advisory Board (SAB), the General Accounting Office (GAO), and many other organizations; in congressional oversight and judicial proceedings; and in countless criticisms and lawsuits from stakeholders with interests in particular EPA regulatory decisions.

As early as 1974, concerns about EPA's scientific mission, research organization, and research planning process were expressed by an NRC committee (NRC 1974). Three years later, a set of important recommendations that eventually helped define some of the principal features of the agency's current research program were made in the NRC report *Analytical Studies for the U.S. Environmental Protection Agency, Volume III: Research and Development in the Environmental Protection Agency* (NRC 1977). Among the recommendations, the 1977 report stated that all EPA research should be centralized in the agency's Office of Research and Development (ORD); that ORD should conduct a mixture of fundamental, anticipatory, and regulatory support research; that an integrated risk-assessment office should be created in ORD; and that an extramural program of research grants and centers should be established. Although those particular recommendations were soon adopted by EPA, other recommendations of the 1977 report were not followed immediately but were adopted nearly 2 decades later (see Chapter 2). For instance, the 1977 report called for a clear definition of EPA's research mission, the development of a strategic plan for environmental research, and nonmanagerial career advancement paths for EPA research scientists.

EPA's own SAB has constructively criticized the agency's scientific performance and recommended changes in the agency's research program many times over the years. Especially important among the SAB reports of recent years were *Future Risk: Research Strategies for the 1990s* (EPASAB 1988) and *Reducing Risk: Setting Priorities and Strategies for*

Environmental Protection (EPASAB 1990). In the 1988 report, the SAB emphasized the need for EPA and its research program to shift emphasis from the traditional command-and-control and cleanup strategies to the anticipation and prevention of pollution problems. Among its recommendations, the 1988 report called for ORD to expand its long-term research program, emphasizing core research areas in which EPA has special capabilities and responsibilities. It also recommended that ORD place greater emphasis on anticipatory studies and monitoring, understanding human exposure to pollutants, and epidemiological research. The 1988 report also urged EPA to increase its efforts in public education, technology transfer, and education of environmental scientists. *Reducing Risk: Setting Priorities and Strategies for Environmental Protection* (EPASAB 1990), stressed the need for EPA and its research program to become more proactive. It argued that EPA and its research program, given limited resources, should move beyond the agency's longstanding practice of fragmented regulatory program responses driven by individual statutory mandates, and move toward a cost-effective focus on the greatest health and environmental risks and the greatest opportunities for reducing those risks. Among its recommendations, the SAB's 1990 report also urged ORD to place greater emphasis on risks to ecosystems and on the development of better risk-assessment methods and data.

In *Safeguarding the Future: Credible Science, Credible Decisions* (EPA 1992), a panel of senior academicians, including two members of this NRC committee, concluded, "Currently, EPA science is of uneven quality, and the Agency's policies and regulations are frequently perceived as lacking a strong scientific foundation." While acknowledging that EPA had a number of knowledgeable scientists on its staff, the panel reported that the science base at EPA was not *perceived* to be strong by the university community, and that many EPA scientists at all levels throughout the agency believed that EPA did not use their scientific knowledge and resources effectively.

The 1992 panel observed, "A perception exists that regulations based on unsound science have led to unneeded economic and social burdens, and that unsound science has sometimes led to decisions that expose people and ecosystems to avoidable risks." The panel commented that EPA had not always ensured that contrasting, reputable scientific views were well-explored and well-documented from the beginning to the end of the regulatory process. It pointed out that the agency was often perceived to have a conflict of interest because it needed science to support its regulatory activities, and the panel described a widely held perception by people both outside and inside the agency that EPA science was "adjusted" by EPA scientists or decision-makers, consciously or unconsciously, to fit policy.

The NRC's Board on Environmental Studies and Toxicology, which oversaw the study that produced this report, has issued many previous reports urging improvements in specific parts of EPA's research program and scientific performance. Examples of such reports are *Rethinking the Ozone Problem in Urban and Regional Air Pollution* (NRC 1991); *Science and Judgment in Risk Assessment* (NRC 1994c); *Review of EPA's Environmental Monitoring and Assessment Program* (NRC 1994a,b, 1995a); *Research Priorities for Airborne Particulate Matter* (NRC 1998a, 1999c); and *Modeling Mobile-Source Emissions* (NRC 2000).

THIS NRC STUDY

In the fiscal year 1995 appropriations report for EPA, Congress directed the agency to obtain an independent assessment from the National Academy of Sciences regarding the overall structure and management of EPA's research program and an evaluation of scientific peer-review procedures used by the agency.

This report is the fourth prepared by two companion expert committees convened by the NRC, the principal operating arm of the National Academy of Sciences and the National Academy of Engineering, in response to that congressional request and to subsequent, related requests from EPA. To carry out the study, the NRC appointed the Committee on Research and Peer Review in EPA, which prepared an interim report (NRC 1995b) addressing the initial request from Congress, according to a short deadline set by Congress, as well as this report, the final report in the study. As part of the study, the NRC also appointed a companion committee—the Committee on Research Opportunities and Priorities for EPA—which issued an interim report in 1996 and the report *Building a Foundation for Sound Environmental Decisions* in 1997 (NRC 1997). This fourth and final report expands on issues discussed in the previous reports and addresses related questions.

The members of both committees were chosen by the NRC for their expertise in biology, chemistry, statistics, chemical engineering, environmental engineering, atmospheric sciences, toxicology, exposure assessment, public health, ecology, soil science, and other disciplines. Special emphasis was placed on selecting committee members with research-management experience and knowledge of the research and other scientific activities of EPA and other agencies. The chairman and two other members of the Committee on Research Opportunities and Priorities for EPA were also members of the Committee on Research and Peer Review in EPA.

The Committee on Research and Peer Review in EPA was charged to assess EPA's overall research-program structure, peer-review procedures, long-term research program, laboratory site-review procedures, and research-staff career-development and performance-evaluation procedures. It was asked to consider problems, issues, and recommendations contained in previous evaluations of EPA's research program and peer-review practices, as well as other relevant problems and issues that the committee might identify. In framing its approach to its task, the committee was asked to place particular emphasis on the aspect of its charge regarding previous evaluations of scientific practices and performance in EPA. Previous evaluations by committees of the NRC, EPA's SAB, and other independent groups are featured prominently in our committee's reports. Many of their findings and recommendations are cited and reviewed in some detail, and we have tried to build on their foundation and to indicate clearly where we did or did not agree with them.

In addition, our committee's approach to its task was strongly influenced by two important developments that occurred during the course of our study. First, in 1996 EPA's ORD requested and obtained under the Federal Advisory Committee Act a charter for a new body, the Board of Scientific Counselors (BOSC), to advise EPA's Assistant Administrator for Research and Development. The BOSC is not part of the SAB but is organized and operates in a similar manner. Established with 15 senior expert members from universities and other organizations serving on an ongoing basis, including one member of our NRC committee, and augmented with temporary members appointed to serve on ad hoc subcommittees as needed, including additional members of our NRC committee, the BOSC is charged to evaluate the management and operations of ORD's research programs and peer-review practices. The BOSC conducts site reviews of ORD's laboratories and centers and evaluations of research staff in ORD, and it has already issued its first round of reviews and evaluations. In Chapter 2 of this report, our committee discusses the results of the BOSC's reviews and evaluations and, for the most part, concludes that we concur with them and that the BOSC should continue to conduct site reviews and staff evaluations. Although additional findings and recommendations of our committee are included in Chapter 2, we mainly decided to endorse and defer to the BOSC on this aspect of the committee's task.

The second important development that affected our committee's approach to its task was the creation in 1996, at EPA's request, of the NRC's Committee on Research Opportunities and Priorities for EPA, our companion committee in this study, as stated above. That committee was charged to provide an overview of significant emerging environmental issues, identify and prioritize research themes most relevant to understanding and resolving those issues, and consider the role of EPA's research program in the context of research being conducted or sponsored by other organizations. In its 1997 report, *Building a Foundation for Sound Environmental Decisions*, our companion committee assessed and re-defined key aspects of the goals and structure of EPA's research program. It replaced previously used terms like "long-term" and "short-term" research, and "basic" and "applied" research, with the concepts of "core" and "problem-driven" research, as discussed in Chapter 2. As stated in that chapter, our committee fully concurs with our companion committee on these issues, so the component of our charge dealing with "long-term" research was re-oriented to be compatible with the new terms and concepts.

During the course of study leading to the preparation of this report, the Committee on Research and Peer Review in EPA drew on the expertise and experience of its members, considered more than 300 relevant documents obtained from EPA and other sources, and consulted with more than 200 scientists, engineers, managers, and other persons within and outside EPA to obtain relevant information and insights on research-program structure, planning, funding, and management; organizational matters; and scientific career development, performance evaluation, recruitment, and morale issues. The committee held seven 2-day plenary meetings, six of them at National Academies facilities in

Washington, DC; Woods Hole, MA; and Irvine, CA; and one meeting at the EPA laboratory facilities in Research Triangle Park, NC. In addition, teams of committee members and staff made one or more site visits to interview agency scientists, managers, and other staff at each of the following EPA laboratories, centers, headquarters offices, and regional offices: National Health and Environmental Effects Research Laboratory, Cincinnati, OH; Corvallis, OR; and Research Triangle Park, NC; National Exposure Research Laboratory, Cincinnati, OH; Las Vegas, NV; and Research Triangle Park, NC; National Risk Management Research Laboratory, Cincinnati, OH; and Research Triangle Park, NC; National Center for Environmental Assessment, Cincinnati, OH; Research Triangle Park, NC; and Washington, DC; National Center for Environmental Research, Washington, DC; Office of the Administrator, Washington, DC; Office of Air and Radiation, Research Triangle Park, NC; and Washington, DC; Office of Policy, Planning and Evaluation, Washington, DC; Office of Prevention, Pesticides, and Toxic Substances, Washington, DC; Office of Research and Development, Washington, DC; Office of Solid Waste and Emergency Response, Washington, DC; Office of Water, Washington, DC; and regional EPA offices in Boston, MA; Chicago, IL; Denver, CO; New York, NY; and San Francisco, CA. At those locations, committee members and staff interviewed a cross section of EPA personnel, including senior officials, middle managers, staff scientists and engineers, and support staff. At each location, the site-visit team posed a prepared list of questions pertaining to the committee's charge. Following the site visits, the responses to the questions were discussed by the committee. During the course of the study, committee members and staff also interviewed officials knowledgeable about EPA from Congress, the GAO, NSF, NIH, the Office of Management and Budget (OMB), and the Office of Science and Technology Policy (OSTP). In addition, some members of the committee have previously served on one or more groups that independently evaluated the research programs of EPA and other federal agencies under the auspices of the NRC, the Carnegie Commission, EPA's SAB, ORD's BOSC, or other organizations.

Shortly before our committee began its work, an EPA agency-wide committee was in the process of internally evaluating the agency's research program. In July 1994, that committee completed its report to the EPA administrator, *Research, Development, and Technical Services at*

EPA: A New Beginning (EPA 1994b). The report recommended major changes in the ORD program, and the agency began implementing them in 1995 (see Chapter 2).

Soon afterward, our committee's interim report (NRC 1995b) offered a preliminary endorsement of the general scope and direction of the changes then being made in ORD, as well as other steps being taken to strengthen agency-wide peer-review practices. A full assessment was not possible at that time, because the changes were a work in progress and needed time to take root. Now, the committee judges the 1995 reorganization of ORD and the agency's new peer-review practices to be essentially in place and, although still a work in progress, sufficiently mature to be assessed in this report.

2

Research Management at EPA

THE ROLE OF ORD

EPA's Office of Research and Development (ORD) conducts research in its in-house laboratories, funds extramural research at academic institutions and other organizations, performs a variety of activities in the development and application of risk-assessment methods and regulatory criteria, and provides technical services in support of the agency's mission and its regulatory and regional offices. In fiscal year 1999, ORD had 1,976 staff members at 12 geographically dispersed laboratory facilities, three field stations, three assessment offices, and the headquarters office in Washington, DC. ORD also had an extramural research budget of about $315 million—more than half of its $559 million total budget in fiscal year 1999—for grants, cooperative and interagency agreements, contracts, and fellowships. Over the past 20 years, the resources of ORD have generally comprised about 7% of the agency's total budget (Figure 2-1).

A great deal of scientific activity is conducted or funded by EPA offices outside ORD. This work is typically labeled as something other than "research." The other offices of EPA do not have the kind of authorization that ORD has to conduct research per se, and full disclosure might risk the loss of control of some of these activities by the regulatory offices. Perhaps the existence of a substantial amount of research-

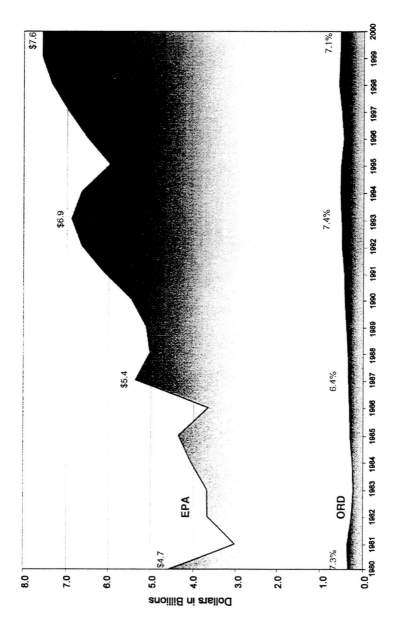

FIGURE 2-1   Comparison of EPA and ORD total budgets, 1980-2000. Source: EPA.

like activity outside ORD is an indication that the agency's regulatory and regional offices believe that ORD is not fully meeting their scientific needs. In any case, it is problematic, because many scientific activities performed or funded outside ORD historically have not been well-coordinated across the agency and have not been included in the ORD research planning and peer-review programs.

In response to a recommendation from our companion committee in this NRC study (NRC 1997), ORD and the EPA Science Policy Council, with the assistance of other EPA offices, began to develop in 1998 an agency-wide "inventory of science activities." The inventory is intended to become an "evergreen" interactive planning tool to integrate a variety of scientific efforts within a common strategy. Organized according to the agency's strategic goals under the Government Performance and Results Act, the inventory holds promise as a tool to help improve scientific collaboration across agency offices and to identify scientific gaps and opportunities for consolidation. The first draft of the inventory is sketchy, containing only general information about the various activities and no information about resources or milestones. It is not yet well-documented or published. Agency work groups are working under the direction of the Science Policy Council to develop recommendations for improvement of the scope, purposes, and form of the inventory, as well as standards for collecting the relevant information.

From time to time, the question arises whether EPA should have its own research program or rely on research results developed elsewhere. Advocates of having the research conducted elsewhere often cite past criticisms of the agency's research program and point to excellent research programs of other agencies and organizations, which collectively, and in some cases individually, dwarf that of EPA. Many other agencies and organizations certainly contribute much of the scientific and technical information that EPA requires. At the federal level, they include the Departments of Agriculture, Commerce, Defense, Energy, and Interior; the NIH; National Aeronautics and Space Administration; and NSF. NSF devotes about $600 million a year to environmental research—about the same as ORD's total budget—and recently, the National Science Board recommended a major expansion of NSF's environmental research, planning, education, and scientific assessment, with a funding target of an additional $1 billion over 5 years (NSF

1999). The Department of Energy spends about $500 million a year on environmental quality research. Many public-health, environmental, and natural-resource agencies at the state and local levels also support scientific activities. Internationally, the World Health Organization, the International Agency for Research on Cancer, and many nations have strong scientific review and risk assessment programs. And, of course, the academic community and the private sector conduct much of the research relevant to EPA's mission.

In *Safeguarding the Future: Credible Science, Credible Decisions* (EPA 1992), a panel of four senior academicians, including two members of our committee, was asked by EPA's then-administrator William Reilly for advice on how the agency could best meet the goal of using sound science for its decision-making. The panel concluded that "EPA needs its own strong science base to provide the background required for effective environmental protection programs." The panel gave several reasons for this conclusion:

- *EPA decisions frequently are controversial and affect broad sectors of society and the economy. Controversial decisions demand a strong science base when decisions are made.*
- *EPA cannot rely only on other government agencies to develop the scientific information it needs for decision-making.*
- *The existence of its own science base allows EPA to tie science to long-term regulatory objectives and other environmental protection strategies.*
- *Interaction between scientists and policy-makers is essential for sound decision-making.*
- *Some scientific activities, such as controlled human exposure studies, require special facilities that are beyond the capability of most university-based research programs.*

The NRC's Committee on Research Opportunities and Priorities for EPA — our companion committee in this study — also concluded that EPA needs a strong in-house research program (NRC 1997).

Based on the extensive experience of members of our committee with the research program and applications of science in EPA (see Chapter 1), our committee agrees that a vigorous research program should be maintained in EPA. Moving the research program out of the agency would most likely weaken, not strengthen, the scientific foundation of EPA's decisions and actions. Although some abstract concept of scientific "quality" might be improved by reducing some kinds of ORD technical work that are unlikely to advance research frontiers, such work is often critically necessary to EPA's pursuit of its mission and statutory responsibilities. Overall, eliminating ORD or moving its functions out of EPA would be destructive, and the level of damage would increase with passing time as EPA became increasingly unable to pursue, apply, or even understand new research knowledge. An EPA devoid of a research program would not be likely to attract substantial scientific talent, and an EPA without the kind of scientific talent that research attracts could be ineffective and potentially harmful to the nation.

However, ORD should recognize its limits and the need to depend on partnerships with other research organizations. ORD's resources are important, but only a small part of the total resources devoted to research relevant to environmental protection in the United States and abroad. Even with a much larger budget, ORD could never meet all of EPA's vast and constantly changing needs for scientific knowledge. ORD has had a first-rate research program in some important areas, such as aquatic toxicology and human inhalation toxicology, but it is not possible for ORD to conduct in-house research across the full range of scientific knowledge required by EPA. If ORD were to try to meet all of EPA's needs for scientific knowledge, it would dilute its research efforts on the most important problems and detract from critical core research needs. Careful choices need to be made in using ORD's important but limited resources to maximize the value it adds to the total reservoir of knowledge that is needed and disseminated within EPA, the scientific community, and other organizations. As recommended in *Future Risk: Research Strategies for the 1990s* (EPASAB 1988) and *Building a Foundation for Sound Environmental Decisions* (NRC 1997), EPA should focus on a few core research areas that it can handle well and rely on partnerships and outreach for other scientific needs.

The agency should strive to stimulate and coordinate research at national and international institutions that is responsive to its needs. EPA should be a leader in some areas of research, involved in others, and well informed in all relevant areas. To accomplish that, EPA needs a cadre of scientists responsible for maintaining a thorough awareness in specific research areas that are important to the mission of the agency. It should develop a strong, structured approach to the retrieval, synthesis, and application of the results of research conducted not only by ORD, but also by scientists not affiliated with or supported by EPA. This includes research conducted or sponsored by other federal and state agencies, universities, and industries, both in this country and abroad. The internet presents great opportunities for enhancing interagency and international research coordination.

Another important question asked from time to time pertains to the overall balance in EPA's research program. In a report accompanying EPA's appropriations for fiscal year 1993, the congressional conference committee requested EPA to review the balance between its basic and applied research, stating, ·

> *The Committee believes that, for a number of reasons, EPA has failed to sufficiently address the issue of basic research. Due to the large number of regulatory and statutory mandates, the Agency has focused on short-term applied research. Basic research can be used to identify and assess environmental problems which pose the greatest risk to human health and the environment.*

ORD's strategic plan (EPA 1996a, 1997a) states, "While all of EPA uses science for policy and regulatory decision-making, and various EPA offices contribute to the scientific underpinnings of the Agency's decisions, the responsibility for leadership in science at EPA and for the bulk of EPA's research and development work resides in the Office of Research and Development." Yet, EPA's statutory mandates and regulatory programs have historically been problem-driven, and consequently so has most of ORD's program. Strong demands are placed on ORD to meet the needs of the agency's regulatory programs.

The difficulties of serving multiple regulatory-office clients while trying to sustain a core-research program have posed challenges to ORD throughout its history. ORD has continually been torn between competing demands: on the one hand, to lead, and on the other hand, to serve the rest of EPA.

EPA acknowledged that difficulty in the preface to *Fundamental and Applied Research at the Environmental Protection Agency* (EPA 1994a):

> *Indeed, the difficulty for EPA as well as for other regulatory agencies has been meeting the needs of many research clients. EPA's research program must strike a balance between providing data and technical*

support for 'front-line' regulators solving environmental problems today and building a science knowledge base necessary to manage our ecological resources wisely in the coming decades; understand how pollutants affect our health; and prevent or reduce environmental risks in the future.

In *Building a Foundation for Sound Environmental Decisions* (NRC 1997), our companion committee in this NRC study recommended that EPA's research program maintain a balance of roughly equal proportions between *problem-driven research*, targeted at understanding and solving particular, identified environmental problems and reducing the uncertainties associated with them, and *core research*, which aims to provide broader, more generic information to help improve understanding relevant to environmental problems for the present and future. It described problem-driven research as the kind of research and technical support activity that ORD has pursued most in the past, efforts that are largely driven by current or anticipated regulatory efforts of other EPA offices. Problem-driven research is a means to understand single problems in depth and assess remedies. Core research is largely aimed at providing knowledge for the agency to anticipate and respond to current and future environmental problems.

The 1997 report described three components of core research:

- Acquiring a systematic understanding of the physical, chemical, biological, geological, social, and economic processes that underlie and drive environmental systems, and the biochemical and physiological processes in humans that are affected by environmental agents.
- Developing broadly applicable research tools and methods for understanding and managing environmental problems, including better techniques for measuring physical, chemical, biological, social, and economic variables of interest; more accurate models of complex systems and their interactions; and new methods for analyzing, displaying, and using environmental information for science-based decision-making.
- Designing, implementing, and maintaining appropriate environmental monitoring programs and evaluating, synthesizing, and disseminating the data and results to improve understanding of the status of and changes in environmental resources

over time and retrospectively evaluating whether environmental policies are having the desired effects.

The distinction between research in problem-driven and core areas is not always clear-cut, and the categories might often overlap. Fundamental discoveries can be made during the search for solutions to narrowly defined problems, and breakthroughs in problem-solving sometimes occur as a result of core-research efforts. Feedback between the two types of research greatly enhances the overall research endeavor. The goals of core research tend not to vary much over time, so core-research priorities will remain relatively constant. Problem-driven research, on the other hand, should be responsive to regulatory program needs and changing priorities, so it should be re-evaluated and refocused regularly.

Our committee concurs with the 1997 NRC report and supports the increased priority and proportion of a core-research program in ORD. The core-research program should endeavor to emphasize the evaluation of potential environmental concerns and "over-the-horizon" possibilities (EPASAB 1995), as well as new approaches to managing current problems.

Safeguards will continue to be needed to ensure that the important scientific needs of EPA's regulatory programs and regional offices are not unduly compromised. A great burden has been placed on the agency-wide strategic-planning process, discussed later in this chapter, to ensure that such compromise does not occur. ORD's technical support role should be planned and conducted with clear understanding of the goals of such support, the appropriate degrees of interaction with program office staff, and the timing and channels of such interactions.

ORD's programs should address the needs of the agency in the context of a broad, comprehensive framework (e.g., Presidential/Congressional Commission on Risk Assessment and Risk Management 1997a,b). Our committee believes that ORD's overall program should

- Identify and define the risks to human health and the environment and develop scientific and technical approaches to reduce such risks.
- Demonstrate the feasibility of regulatory or nonregulatory risk-reduction actions that may be taken.

- Support and facilitate the development and implementation of necessary regulations aimed at reducing risk.

Both the problem-driven and core components of EPA's research serve to support EPA's fundamental mission: to identify, assess, and abate risks to public health and the environment. Viewed in that context, the strategic mission of EPA's research program, in both the short and long run, is to develop and advance the scientific and technical basis for risk identification and assessment and to guide decision-makers in making risk-management judgments and selecting overall priorities.

Many scientists within and outside the agency believe that ORD should become more of a pro-active leader for the rest of the agency, giving greater emphasis to anticipatory research that develops the knowledge to lead EPA into new strategies and levels of understanding. Regulatory officials, on the other hand, often argue that EPA's limited resources, including ORD's, are provided to support the agency's existing statutory mandates and regulatory programs, so ORD should provide the regulatory offices with more technical assistance and short-term, quick-payoff, applied work.

Our committee is convinced, as was our companion committee (NRC 1997), that the core-research role is of crucial importance to EPA and the nation. The very nature of the problems faced by EPA has been changing dramatically, and surprises have become common. EPA was created in 1970 with the limited understanding of environmental issues available at that time, including some concepts that are now largely outdated and rapidly being subsumed in new concepts such as sustainable development and industrial ecology (EPASAB 1988; NAE 1994; NAPA 1994; OSTP 1994). These concepts envision the integration of environmental science and technology throughout the entire economy. They are not simply (or in many cases even primarily) concerned with reducing existing impacts or ensuring compliance with so-called "end-of-pipe" regulations. If ORD is to participate effectively in developing and implementing new concepts and policy directions, its scope of activities should be appropriately expansive. ORD should address not only the individual pollution-related problems that have traditionally concerned EPA, but also the research on complex topics such as sustainable development and biological diversity. Research should lead the activities of EPA and not just follow past policies or respond to currently perceived needs. EPA's research should address future problems, not just past and present problems.

Some research problems are sufficiently broad or complex that they can be addressed effectively only by a long-term focused effort. In addition, a sustained program of anticipatory research would be expected to reduce the need for reactive projects in many cases. An effective over-the-horizon research program seeks to anticipate and address future scientific needs in support of environmental protection, thereby reducing future needs for reactive efforts that are often less efficient and more expensive.

Using ORD for short-term scientific assistance to regulatory and regional offices has some undeniably important benefits. Perhaps the greatest dividends are the resulting improvements in the scientific aspects of regulations, the maintenance of an in-house scientific core group experienced in dealing with environmental risks and programs, and the knowledge of agency issues that the research scientists obtain through such experience. An experienced scientific core group can be of great importance in meeting emergency requirements for scientific expertise. ORD's technical assistance provides the regulatory offices with competent scientific support, and it enables the ORD research scientists to keep abreast of regulatory and policy developments elsewhere in EPA.

ORD should meet the continuing challenge to lead the agency through research while continuing to assist its client regulators, who have variable levels of understanding and appreciation of science but a strong say in ORD's budget and priorities. ORD's regulatory assistance activities often have a narrow focus and compete with or preempt long-term research programs. Such activities tend to consume the resources of a research organization disruptively as well as disproportionately. There is also some inevitable risk to ORD's scientific credibility when it provides technical assistance for regulatory strategies that might be predetermined, or are perceived to be. In addition, regulatory strategies, which are typically prescriptive and specific, tend to freeze concepts and methods in time. The scientific components of regulations also tend to be frozen in time. The more closely that ORD is tied to the regulatory programs, the greater the risk that ORD will work to some extent on outdated problems or with outdated approaches — waging the last war instead of preparing for the next one.

THE 1995 REORGANIZATION OF ORD

By the early 1990s, the structure of ORD reflected its historical origins, the traditional areas of strength of its laboratories, the technical-assistance requirements of the agency's regulatory programs, directives from Congress, the agency's research-mission ambiguities, and a culture of entrepreneurship in some parts of ORD. In 1993, EPA estimated that approximately 29% of ORD's total resources were devoted to "fundamental" research, 43% to "application-directed" research, 19% to "development," and 9% to "technical assistance," although it expressed uncertainty about how to define those terms (EPA 1993).

As our committee began its work, EPA was making major changes in its research program. The process leading to those changes began in 1993 with a decision by the administrator, in response to a request of Congress, to evaluate all of EPA's laboratories in relation to the agency's scientific and technical needs. The first major step in the evaluation was a study by the MITRE Corporation, working with a team of EPA officials, and with assessments by EPA's Science Advisory Board (SAB) and the National Academy of Public Administration (NAPA). The MITRE (1994) report, *A Comprehensive Study of EPA Scientific and Technical Laboratories and Their Facilities and Capabilities*, provided extensive documentation on the laboratories and their functions, as well as an analysis of five principal options for reorganizing them. Among its findings, the MITRE report expressed concern about the lack of clear, agreed-upon mission statements for EPA, ORD, or the laboratories. It also commented on the excessive use of contract personnel at EPA laboratories, various facility and equipment problems, and the need for improvement in quality-assurance and research-planning practices. Regarding laboratory reorganization, the MITRE report concluded that the discipline-based organization of ORD's laboratories was not optimal to support the mission-based organization of the rest of the agency. It favored a functional reorganization as previously recommended in *Environmental Research and Development - Strengthening the Federal Infrastructure* (Carnegie Commission on Science, Technology, and Government 1992).

EPA's SAB and the NAPA reviewed the MITRE report (NAPA 1994; EPASAB 1994). The SAB report generally concurred with MITRE in endorsing a variation of the Carnegie Commission model for laboratory organization, but it argued that management improvements were needed in ORD before reorganization should occur. The SAB expressed concern about the extent to which EPA laboratory scientists were being required to serve as contract managers. It also expressed concern about the possibility that decreased ORD involvement in short-term, applied research and technical assistance to the regulatory and regional offices might lead to the expansion of separate research programs in the regulatory offices, potentially damaging the overall quality and effectiveness of ORD's research role in the agency. The NAPA review also generally supported the MITRE recommendations but emphasized that ORD's mission and goals should be clarified before any laboratory reorganization took place.

In response to the MITRE study and the SAB and NAPA reviews, an agency-wide, senior-level steering committee prepared final recommendations to the administrator. Its report, *Research, Development, and Technical Services at EPA: A New Beginning* (EPA 1994b), recommended the following changes in ORD's research program:

Strategic Planning: Initiate a new strategic research planning process in concert with other offices of EPA.

The Role(s) of ORD: Increase long-term research from about 30% to at least 50% of ORD's total program budget.

ORD's Laboratories: Functionally consolidate ORD's 12 laboratories, three field stations, and four assessment centers into three national laboratories and a national assessment center, thereby delegating more research-management responsibility to the laboratories. Reduce Washington, DC headquarters staff of ORD by half through attrition and reassignment. Replace some contract personnel at EPA laboratories with federal personnel. Establish new scientific career-track opportunities and performance-evaluation procedures for EPA laboratory scientists.

Research Grants: Increase annual funding for extramural, investigator-initiated, peer-reviewed, competitive research grants and centers from $20 million to $100 million. Create a competitive, investigator-initiated research-grants program for in-house scientists at ORD's laboratories.

Peer Review: Strengthen and expand peer-review practices for proposals, publications, risk assessments, and laboratory programs.

Fellowships: Create a program of 300 graduate-student fellowships.

The EPA administrator accepted those recommendations, and the actions taken in response to them amounted to the most important changes in the history of ORD.

ORD stated four main goals of the 1995 reorganization (EPA 1996a):

- To reorganize and refocus its laboratories and other organizational components using risk assessment and risk management as organizing principles.
- To increase its interactions with the academic community by expanding its competitive extramural research grants and fellowship programs.
- To expand and strengthen its peer-review practices.
- To institute a new strategic planning process for setting research priorities.

In addition, ORD decided to delegate some laboratory-management and administrative authority from headquarters to the laboratories, giving more decision-making responsibility to laboratory managers and eliminating a layer of headquarters administrators. Although the missions of individual laboratories were adjusted, no ORD laboratory facility was abolished in the reorganization. Each former laboratory director simply began to report to the director of a newly designated national laboratory instead of an ORD suboffice director at headquarters. The directors of the national laboratories report directly to the assistant administrator for research and development. The headquarters suboffices to which the laboratory directors previously reported were abolished, and ORD reduced its headquarters staff substantially through reorganization and attrition.

ORD has stated (EPA 1996a) that the most important strategic principle guiding the 1995 reorganization and refocusing of its program was the risk-assessment and risk-management paradigm developed by committees of the National Academy of Sciences (NRC 1983, 1994c), as summarized in Figure 2-2. Figure 2-3 illustrates some of the most important ways in which scientific and technical activities potentially contribute to the process of risk management.

FIGURE 2-2.   Risk-assessment and risk-management paradigm. Source: EPA 1996a.

The new risk-based organization of ORD is summarized in Figure 2-4. In recommending this reorganization, the *New Beginning* report (EPA 1994b) identified the following benefits and limitations:

Benefits
- Aligns laboratory missions with EPA's unique research responsibilities for reducing uncertainty associated with risk assessment, with research priorities directly related to needs of the environmental management decision process.
- Focuses missions to provide a clear framework for determining the appropriate composition of the scientific work force and supports development of required critical mass of key scientific and engineering disciplines.
- Permits organization of ORD research on a multi-media, multi-stressor basis involving human and ecological risks.
- Enables the agency to better identify where cooperation and joint activities with other federal agencies, industry, and academia can yield sufficient gains.
- Moves laboratory leadership to the field and creates necessary conditions to empower laboratory directors and federal scientific teams.

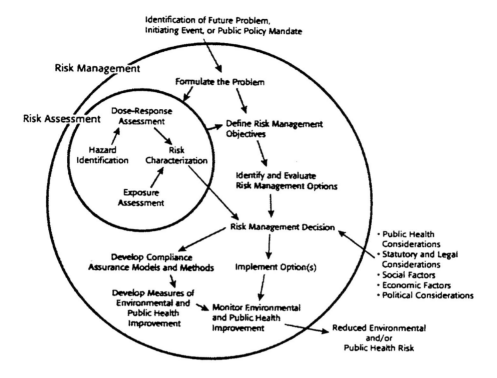

FIGURE 2-3   Scientific and technical contributions to risk management. Source: EPA 1996a.

- Creates opportunities to build new working relationships between ORD and its clients.
- Creates the opportunity for greater scientific career development in the staff.

Limitations
- Science leadership and innovation by national laboratories must be guided by a strengthened research planning and decision process that includes effective participation of program and regional offices in establishing needs, priorities, and accountability.
- Processes must be established to support laboratory based science leaders, allowing them to interact effectively in national and international policy and science forums.

50

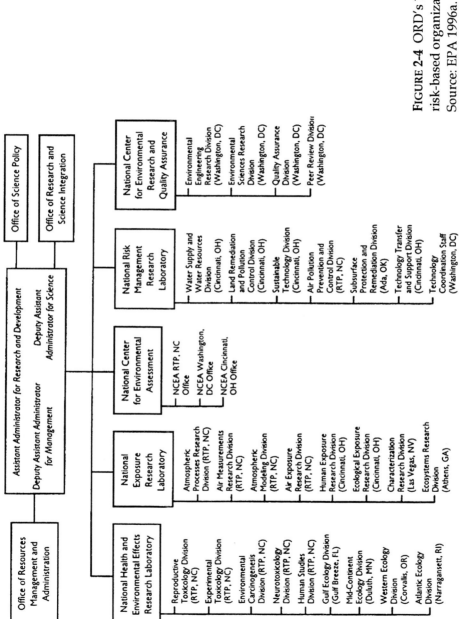

FIGURE 2-4 ORD's 1995 risk-based organization. Source: EPA 1996a.

Restructuring the ORD laboratories according to the risk-assessment paradigm was intended to ensure that research programs within the laboratories would focus their strengths on reducing the uncertainties in identifying, understanding, and managing environmental risks. Such a focus for the in-house EPA laboratories was also recommended by the SAB (EPASAB 1988). Emphasis on reducing the uncertainties in risk assessment was previously recommended in *Safeguarding the Future: Credible Science, Credible Decisions* (EPA 1992), and a 1994 NRC report later defined such uncertainties and variability more fully (NRC 1994c). Although the missions and scientific requirements of EPA and ORD are far broader in scope than the risk-assessment paradigm, ORD chose to focus its in-house laboratories on areas of research related to the aspects of risk assessment and risk management (e.g., aquatic toxicology, inhalation toxicology, control technology) that historically have been of greatest interest to EPA and its laboratories and are not high priorities for research in other agencies. Other research areas would mainly be supported through partnerships with other agencies and organizations, including ORD's extramural grants program. With the restructuring of the ORD research enterprise, it was considered essential that ORD laboratory personnel be capable of performing state-of-the-art research techniques, that they take leadership roles in national and international environmental research initiatives, and that they interact effectively with those components of EPA that need technical information.

Before 1995, roughly 30% of ORD's resources were devoted to what ORD called fundamental and anticipatory research. Since 1995, ORD has increased that proportion to nearly 50%. That increase has resulted in a corresponding reduction in the short-term applied projects and technical assistance that ORD provides for the agency's regulatory offices. In our committee's site visits (see Chapter 1), some complaints were heard from regulatory offices that perceived some reductions in technical support from ORD.

In our 1995 interim report, this committee endorsed ORD's move to focus on reducing uncertainties in risk assessment (also see NRC 1994c and Presidential/Congressional Commission on Risk Assessment and Risk Management 1997a,b) but cautioned that its success would depend critically on the effectiveness of the strategic-planning process. To coordinate research planning and management in the new organization, ORD created several cross-cutting groups (Figure 2-5), including a Research Coordination Council that includes representatives from the agency's regulatory program and regional offices, an Executive Council of laboratory and center directors, a Management Council of deputy laboratory and center directors, a Science Council of assistant laboratory and center directors, and Research Coordination Teams involving assistant laboratory and center directors (Figure 2-5).

Our interim report also offered a preliminary endorsement of the general scope and direction of other changes then being made in ORD; a more confident assessment was not possible at that time, because the changes needed time to take root. Now, the committee views the 1995 reorganization of ORD and the agency's peer-review practices to be still a work in progress but sufficiently mature to be assessed in the following pages.

RESEARCH PLANNING

One of the principal findings in *Safeguarding the Future: Credible Science, Credible Decisions* (EPA 1992) was that "EPA does not have a coherent science agenda and operational plan to guide scientific efforts throughout the agency and support its focus on relatively high-risk environmental problems." The authors of that report (including two members of this NRC committee) singled out two areas that especially suffered from the lack of an adequate research planning process and the dominance of the annual budget process in setting the agency's scientific agenda. First, the panel noted that today's increasingly complex environmental problems require greater emphasis on cross-media approaches, whereas the budget process was largely driven by media-specific statutes and priorities. Second, the panel expressed concern that the lack of an adequate scientific planning process had prevented EPA from carrying out prolonged research or anticipating future scientific information needs. It noted that the only certain prediction for the future is that an environmental issue of critical importance that no one has anticipated will appear, so EPA should have a strong science base and flexibility to deal with unanticipated problems. However, it observed that EPA's science programs were not structured to allow for the stable funding needed to pursue the necessary long-term, anticipatory research and scientific assessment.

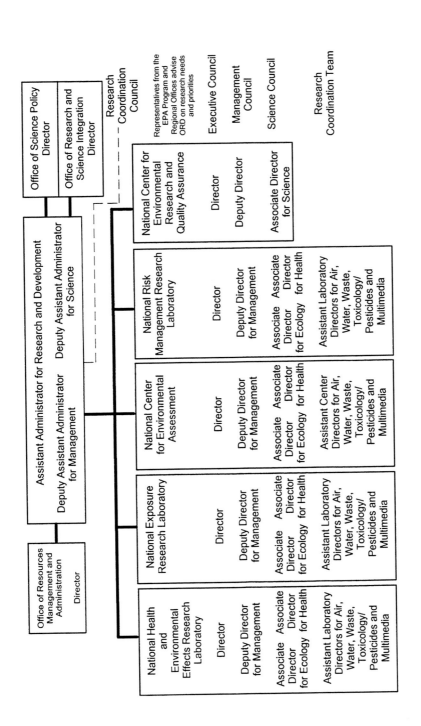

FIGURE 2-5   ORD management structure.   Source: EPA 1996a.

The 1992 *Credible Science* panel judged the EPA budget process to be an "obstacle to formulating and carrying out a coherent science strategy," and it stated that EPA cannot present Congress with a rational argument for an appropriate funding level for science without first developing a coherent strategic plan for its science efforts. The panel recommended that EPA strengthen its strategic scientific planning process and that a comprehensive, long-term scientific strategy drive its annual budget decisions (not vice versa).

Stronger coordination and planning of environmental research among U.S. agencies and greater outreach and research collaboration with other organizations in this country and abroad were also among the principal recommendations of *Environmental Research and Development - Strengthening the Federal Infrastructure* (Carnegie Commission on Science, Technology, and Government 1992) and *Research to Protect, Restore, and Manage the Environment* (NRC 1993).

Over the years, ORD has published several research outlook reports, and just before the 1995 reorganization, ORD was engaged in an "issue-based planning process" (EPA 1993), organized around a selected set of 38 environmental problems and scientific questions, grouped into 12 broad research themes. However, those efforts mainly consisted of describing selected research topics and did not contain the essential elements of a strategic-planning process.

In 1995, our committee's interim report (NRC 1995b) recommended the following in regard to scientific planning in EPA:

Most sorely needed are a coherent scientific and technical strategy statement for EPA, a strategic plan for ORD, and a strategic plan for each ORD laboratory and center that is consistent with the agency and ORD plans. Each strategic plan should consist at a minimum of a vision statement, a mission statement, and a plan for achieving them. These documents need not be lengthy or complex, but they should be robust and specific enough to enable the agency and this committee to evaluate the intended role of ORD and its organizational components in providing scientific and technical knowledge to support national environmental programs, policies, and decisions, as well as to identify unnecessary geographical and functional duplication and significant gaps in ORD activities. It is crucially important that the strategic-planning process drive the development of ORD's budget, instead of being driven by it.

In 1997, as part of its response to the 1993 Government Performance and Results Act, the agency published the *EPA Strategic Plan* (EPA 1997b), which included the broad scientific goals described in the first chapter of this report. In connection with that agency-wide effort, ORD undertook a major effort to institute a new strategic-planning process, as recommended in the *New Beginning* report (EPA 1994b) and the 1995 interim report from our committee (NRC 1995b). A new high-level position, deputy assistant administrator for science, was created to manage the planning process. ORD published a strategic plan in 1996 and an updated plan in 1997. To develop and update its strategic plan, ORD instituted a process involving extensive consultation with all components of ORD, the other offices of EPA, the SAB, the NRC, and others from the private sector and the academic community. Described as a "living" document, the strategic plan (Figure 2-6) defined ORD's vision, mission, strategic principles, long-term goals and objectives, high-priority research topics, and potential measures for judging the success of the program.

The ORD strategic plan (EPA 1996a, 1997a) set forth a simple vision: "ORD will provide the scientific foundation to support EPA's mission." It defined ORD's mission in four statements:

- *Perform research and development to identify, understand, and solve current and future environmental problems.*
- *Provide responsive technical support to EPA's mission.*
- *Integrate the work of ORD's scientific partners (other agencies, nations, private sector organizations, and academia).*
- *Provide leadership in addressing emerging environmental issues and in advancing the science and technology of risk assessment and risk management.*

The plan set forth nine strategic principles for ORD:

- *Focus research and development on the greatest risks to people and the environment, taking into account their potential severity, magnitude, and uncertainty.*
- *Focus research on reducing uncertainty in risk assessment and on cost-effective approaches for preventing and managing risks.*
- *Balance human health and ecological research.*

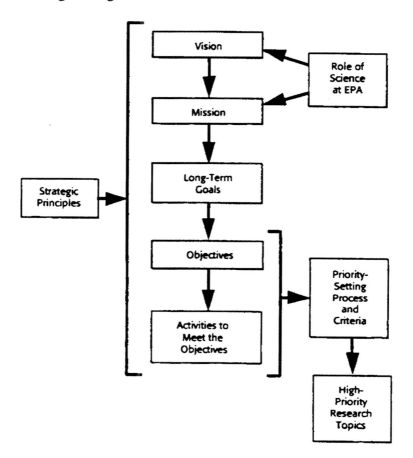

FIGURE 2-6   ORD's strategic plan. Source: EPA 1996a.

- *Infuse ORD's work with a customer/client ethic that breaks down organizational barriers and ensures responsiveness to ORD's internal and external customers.*
- *Give priority to maintaining strong and viable scientific and engineering core capabilities that allow us to conduct an intramural research and technical support program in areas of highest risk and greatest importance to the Agency.*
- *Through an innovative and effective human resources development program, nurture and support the development of outstanding scientists, engineers, and other environmental professionals at EPA.*

- *Take advantage of the creativity of the nation's best research institutions by increasing competitively-awarded research grants to further EPA's critical environmental research mission.*
- *Ensure the quality of the science that underlies our risk assessment and risk reduction efforts by requiring the very highest level of independent peer review and quality assurance for all our science products and programs.*
- *Provide the infrastructure required for ORD to achieve and maintain an outstanding research and development program in environmental science.*

And it proposed six long-term overarching goals for ORD:

- *To develop scientifically sound approaches to assessing and characterizing risks to human health and the environment.*
- *To integrate human health and ecological assessment methods into a comprehensive multimedia assessment methodology.*
- *To provide common sense and cost-effective approaches for preventing and managing risks.*
- *To provide credible, state-of-the-art risk assessments, methods, models, and guidance.*
- *To exchange reliable scientific, engineering, and risk assessment/risk management information among private and public stakeholders.*
- *To provide leadership and encourage others to participate in identifying emerging environmental issues, characterizing the risks associated with these issues, and developing ways of preventing or reducing these risks.*

More-detailed sets of objectives for each of those goals are described in the plan.

ORD's strategic plan recognizes that there will never be sufficient funding to investigate every identified environmental problem, and that there is a need for a systematic basis for organizing its research enterprise and setting priorities among the many research topics that ORD could address. The approach adopted was based on risk magnitude and risk-reduction opportunity.

The 1996 plan and its 1997 update described a research priority-setting process (Figure 2-7) and criteria (Figure 2-8). The process of selecting high-priority research topics involves consultation with sources

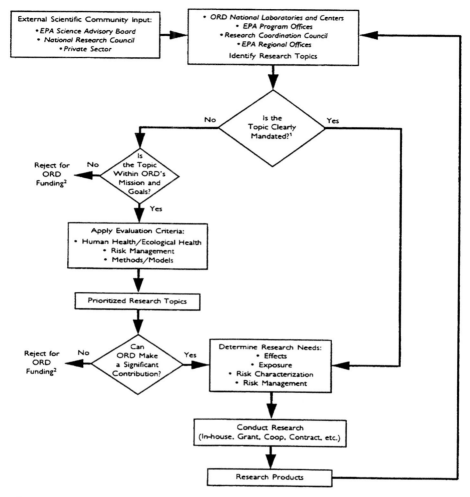

FIGURE 2-7   Setting research priorities. Source: EPA 1996a.

within and outside EPA, followed by assessments of the importance of various research areas to EPA's mission, the risk-assessment and risk-management criteria under consideration, and other factors.

Our committee agrees that EPA's research and development program should focus on scientific and technical areas where there is the

Methods/Models Criteria

- How broadly applicable is the proposed method or model expected to be?
- To what extent will the proposed method or model facilitate or improve risk assessment or risk management?
- How large is the anticipated user community for the proposed method or model?

Risk Management Criteria

- Have the problem's source(s) and risk been characterized sufficiently to develop risk management options?
- Do risk management options (political, legal, socioeconomic, or technical) currently exist? If so, are they acceptable to stakeholders, implementable, reliable, and cost-effective?
- Could new or improved technical solutions prevent or mitigate the risk efficiently, cost-effectively, and in a manner acceptable to stakeholders?
- Are other research organizations (e.g., agencies, industry) currently investigating/ developing these solutions or interested in working in partnership with ORD on these solutions?

Apply when appropriate

Apply when appropriate

Human Health and Ecological Health Criteria

- What type of effect would the research investigate/mitigate and how severely might this effect impact humans or ecosystems?
- Over what time scale might this effect occur?
- How easily can the effect be reversed, and will it be passed on to future generations?
- What level of human or ecological organization would be impacted by the effect?
- On what geographic scale might this effect impact humans or ecosystems?

FIGURE 2-8 ORD criteria for evaluating and ranking potential research topics. Source: EPA. 1996a.

greatest potential for reducing adverse impacts on human health and the environment. This strategy is appropriate in terms of EPA's mission. It will help enable EPA to control or minimize risks as efficiently as possible while focusing the limited resources of the agency and the nation on situations where the pollution has the greatest impact and where the greatest reductions of risk can be expected.

Risk-based prioritization is an appropriate way for ORD to focus many of its in-house research efforts and set priorities among identified environmental problems to investigate. However, risk assessment has important limits as a tool for priority setting. It is still a relatively new concept, and its methodology is still maturing. It tends to be most useful for problems that are well defined and data-rich, and less useful for future or emerging problems that are not yet well defined. There is not as yet any objective way to compare fundamentally different outcomes, such as comparing cancer with non-cancer effects or adverse human-health effects with ecological or property damage. Comparing voluntary with involuntary risks and short-term impacts with future effects are also problematic. Further, present techniques for characterizing the adverse effects of chemical mixtures or other multiple stressors are primitive and inexact.

Applying the process and criteria in its 1996 strategic plan and 1997 update, ORD selected six high-priority research topics and six other important research areas to receive special attention over the following few years within the broader ORD program, and it described potential research tasks, products, and uses for each of the topics and areas in the strategic plan. Of the six highest-priority topics chosen, three are targeted at specific environmental problem areas — safe drinking water, with an initial focus on microbial pathogens, disinfection by-products, and arsenic; high-priority air pollutants, with an initial focus on particulate matter; and emerging environmental issues, with an initial focus on endocrine disruptors. The other three high-priority topics address broader questions of methodology and approaches — research to improve ecosystem risk assessment; research to improve health risk assessment; and research on pollution prevention and new technologies for environmental protection. In fiscal year 1999, ORD devoted about $343 million — a little more than 61% of its total resources of $559 million — to these six high-priority research categories:

Safe Drinking Water	$45.9 million
Particulate Matter	$56.1 million
Endocrine Disruptors	$12.1 million
Ecosystem Risk Assessment	$110.9 million
Health Risk Assessment	$49.5 million
Pollution Prevention	$68.3 million

Additional areas discussed in the 1996 strategic plan and the 1997 update as being important, but not of the highest priority, included research on tropospheric ozone, airborne toxicants, and other air pollutants; indoor air quality; contaminated groundwater, soils, and sediments; exposures to pesticides and toxic substances; waste-site risk characterization; waste management and site remediation; and environmental monitoring. The strategic plan also emphasized the importance of anticipatory research, exploratory research, and other continuing efforts to identify emerging issues, as the SAB had urged in its 1995 report *Beyond the Horizon: Using Foresight to Protect the Environmental Future* (EPASAB 1995).

In its strategic plan, ORD described in general terms the steps involved in translating strategic-planning decisions into a research program. These steps involve the development of research plans; the determination of who should conduct the work (beginning with choices between in-house or extramural investigation); the development of budget operating plans and laboratory implementation plans for in-house work or appropriate extramural mechanisms, such as grants, cooperative agreements, or contracts; and the process of planning for research-information management.

Our committee commends ORD for the progress it has made to date in developing its strategic and research plans. However, we believe that there can be further substantial improvements.

Decision Making

Although the ORD strategic plan discusses the processes and criteria by which decisions are made on research priorities, funding allocations, and who will do the work (in-house or outside the agency), the plan describes the decision-making processes and criteria only in very broad terms. The plan lists several factors that are typically considered when ORD decides who will perform each research activity. These factors include the nature of the work, who has the appropriate expertise, how urgently the results are needed, the degree to which the work must be specified or can be made flexible, the available in-house capacity, the potential value of involving multiple institutions, and the opportunities for funding leverage. ORD has a number of mechanisms available for extramural funding, including interagency agreements, contracts, grants, cooperative agreements, and fellowships. Each of the mechanisms has its own features, advantages, and limitations. The process by which ORD decides whether a project or task is to be performed by in-house staff or through one or more of its extramural mechanisms is of crucial importance to the quality of the work and the cost-effective management of resources. Unfortunately, the descriptions of ORD's decision-making process are inadequate for most persons outside ORD to reconstruct or review the decision-making process. Our committee urges ORD to make processes of priority setting, resource allocation, and intramural or extramural decision-making more transparent and better documented to give the decisions greater credibility to the broad range of stakeholders within and outside the agency.

ORD's strategic plan also discusses the criteria that ORD will use in providing "technical support," which ORD defines as "activities ORD conducts in response to specific requests by the Program Offices, Regions, or states to address well-defined needs that are not covered by ORD's research program." Decisions to allocate ORD funds to technical support are generally based on the potential value of such work to the agency's regulatory programs, the extent to which ORD has unique scientific or technical capabilities to address the problem, the potential benefits to environmental quality and human health relative to the resource requirements for technical support, and the extent to which ORD judges it can help solve the problem. Again, ORD's description of the decision-making process for technical assistance is somewhat vague.

During the committee's site visits and interviews, the staff of some EPA regulatory program offices expressed concern that ORD's support of their programs appears to have diminished since the 1995 reorganization. Some of the program-office staff expressed the concern that, in practice, they have little influence on ORD's research priorities through the Research Coordination Council or any other mechanism. They felt that they need a stronger voice in the setting of ORD's priorities, and that ORD should be held more accountable to the agency's other offices for performing agreed upon tasks. Some program-office staff members also expressed the concern that ORD's performance is often too slow to meet the needs of other EPA offices. As a result, they acknowledged to the committee that EPA regulatory offices engage in some research without ORD involvement, even though those other offices are unable to afford much research.

Dissemination and Technology Transfer

Safeguarding the Future: Credible Science, Credible Decisions (EPA 1992) concluded that the academic community, Congress, other federal agencies, industry, the public, and even many persons within EPA are generally unfamiliar with the work of EPA scientists. The 1992 panel emphasized that many officials involved in funding EPA science were uncertain about what science products EPA had produced, and whether the quality and quantity of its products were commensurate with the dollars expended. It noted that EPA's policy and regulatory work receives a great deal of public attention, but the agency's science typically receives a similar degree of attention only when the scientific basis for a decision is questioned. The panel concluded that EPA should strive to make more widely known the short-term and long-term scientific goals and achievements of its research laboratories, contractors, and grantees. It urged the agency to develop and implement a coherent communications, outreach, and education plan to publicize the activities and accomplishments of EPA scientists.

Even within the agency, many regulatory and regional program officials throughout EPA's history have been largely unaware and even dubious of any important benefits from ORD's research program, and consequently they have not been supportive of ORD's budget. ORD's ongoing efforts to disseminate its research products and inform others about them have, with some exceptions, been meager and unimaginative.

The committee recommends that ORD substantially increase its dissemination and technology-transfer activities. ORD should publish a comprehensive annual summary of its in-house and extramural research and technical-support activities, emphasizing the results and potential applications of its work by other EPA offices, state agencies, industry, and others. ORD should also take stronger measures to assist its stakeholders within and outside the agency to understand and apply the results of ORD's work. ORD should strive harder in demonstrating its accomplishments and anticipated accomplishments to its stakeholders both within and outside the agency.

At the same time, the committee noted during its site visits and interviews with managers and staff of EPA's regulatory offices that not a single individual was in favor of moving the research program outside the agency or even moving the scientific and technical-service functions and resources from ORD to the control of the regulatory program offices. Each group of regulatory officials was asked that question, and the predominant answer was that such moves would weaken, not strengthen, the scientific foundation of EPA's actions and decisions. They considered it highly unlikely that the regulatory offices could ever attract and maintain the high level of staff expertise that ORD has assembled, and even in their worst criticisms of ORD, they believed that a research program outside EPA would be even less helpful than ORD to their needs. Instead, the regulatory officials urged that ORD find a way to become more relevant, helpful, and accountable, at least with respect to the technical services and short-term, problem-driven research components of ORD's program.

Research Plans and Strategies

As promised, ORD has published and continues to publish peer-reviewed plans related to individual high-priority research topics and certain other key research areas. It has published research plans for microbial pathogens and disinfection by-products in drinking water (EPA 1997c), arsenic in drinking water (EPA 1998b), endocrine disruptors (EPA 1998c), and pollution prevention (EPA 1998e), as well as research strategies for particulate-matter research (EPA 1996b), ecological research (EPA 1998d) and waste-management research (EPA 1999a). Each plan has been externally peer reviewed.

Members of our committee reviewed and discussed the research plans and strategies cited above. In general, the committee concludes that these plans are a useful step in the development of ORD's research-planning process. The committee was especially encouraged to note that many of the research priorities described in ORD's research plans for arsenic in drinking water (EPA 1998b) and endocrine disruptors (EPA 1998c) were independently confirmed in similar recommendations published by the NRC in subsequent reports on those topics (NRC 1999a,b). In other words, before receiving the reports from the independent expert committees of the NRC, ORD and its peer-review process arrived at many of the same scientific conclusions. Our committee considers that to be a noteworthy validation of these ORD research-planning efforts.

The committee finds that these and future plans and strategies can be substantially improved, however. Some of the plans (e.g., endocrine disruptors, waste-management research) failed to consider explicitly a substantial amount of research conducted or funded by other agencies and organizations. The plans and strategies contained little information about the resource levels required and measurable results or timetables associated with the anticipated research. The plans and strategies generally give little insight as to how the research activities will be orchestrated and coordinated among ORD laboratories and other agencies and organizations. The basis for setting research priorities is not clearly described in any plan. The plans do not devote much attention to workforce skill mix, facilities, equipment, or data management requirements.

However, the plans and strategies that our committee reviewed are a promising beginning. Other plans under development by ORD will address research on risks to children, mercury, global change, environmental monitoring and assessment, human health risk assessment, and the drinking-water contaminants candidate list.

In 1997, a draft of EPA's particulate-matter research-needs document was reviewed by the Clean Air Scientific Advisory Committee (CASAC) of EPA's SAB (EPASAB 1997). Although ORD's strategic plan (EPA 1996a) emphasized the importance of using research to reduce uncertainties in risk assessment, and the particulate-matter research document also listed that as ORD's top criterion for identifying research needs, the CASAC review concluded that the document failed to identify — or in some cases even acknowledge — the many significant uncertainties about the relationships between airborne particulate matter and health risks, and it failed to place the stated research needs in the context of such uncertainties. The CASAC also expressed doubt about the technical feasibility of some of the research proposed in the EPA document.

Shortly thereafter, at the request of Congress, the NRC convened the Committee on Research Priorities for Airborne Particulate Matter to assist EPA in developing its research strategy in this area. In its first report (NRC 1998), the committee provided a conceptual framework for an integrated national program of particulate-matter research, identified 10 critical research needs linked to key policy-related scientific uncertainties, and proposed a 13-year, integrated research strategy with recommended short-term and long-term timing and estimated costs. In its second report (NRC 1999c), the committee commended EPA on its responsive implementation of the committee's recommendations. Some of the concepts and practices recommended for the particulate-matter research area might help ORD improve its research-planning activities in other areas of research. For example, in 1999, ORD began a pilot effort to translate several of its research strategies and plans for certain areas into multiyear implementation plans, as the NRC had recommended and demonstrated for particulate-matter research. ORD's previous practice had been to plan and implement all research on a year-by-year basis. The multiyear planning should enable ORD and reviewers of the plans to better evaluate research activities, anticipated products, and critical paths over time scales more relevant to a research program than annual projections.

Accountability

Recently, the U.S. General Accounting Office (GAO) criticized ORD's performance in reporting the progress of some of the other research plans listed above, noting that one of the agency's regulatory program offices so acutely needed information on ORD's work, well beyond what ORD was providing, that the regulatory office paid for the development of a system to track ORD's work. The GAO (1999) report stated,

Because the program office needed better information to monitor the status of the work laid out in the research plan and to track project-level resource expenditures, the Office of Water developed its own tracking system for the research on microbial pathogens, disinfectants, and disinfection by-products. Since 1997, the Office of Water has paid a contractor over $148,000 to develop and maintain the tracking system and input data on the status of individual [ORD] projects.

Commenting further on the lack of transparency and progress reporting in ORD's research planning and budgeting process, the GAO report stated,

. . . in commenting on [ORD's] fiscal year 2000 budget, the [SAB's] Research Strategies Advisory Committee indicated that the lack of transparency in the process used to set research priorities made it difficult for the Committee to evaluate the adequacy of the proposed budget. The Committee recommended that EPA make available information on high-ranking programs that it entertained during the budget-making process but could not fund because of overall budget constraints and competition with other programs. In addition, the Committee found that the criteria that EPA used to emphasize or de-emphasize programs in the proposed budget were unclear and recommended that EPA develop explicit criteria that can be used for setting research priorities during the budget development process. The Committee concluded that such an exercise would not only improve communication and understanding of the budget process for those outside the agency, but would also assist EPA in making its internal decision process more efficient.

To address these concerns, the GAO report recommended

First, to improve the link between research needs and resources and to better ensure that limited research funds within EPA and other organizations are most efficiently targeted, we recommended that EPA (1) identify the specific research that must be accomplished, (2) establish time frames showing when the results must be available, (3) estimate the resources that will be required to support the needed research, and (4) use these data to develop budget requests and inform stakeholders about what research will be funded. Second, we recommended that EPA im-

prove the tracking of ongoing research in relation to existing research plans and communicate the agency's progress so that the Office of Research and Development's key customers, including the Office of Water and outside stakeholders, can obtain timely and accurate reports on the status, timing, and funding of individual research projects.

Strategic Planning

The Government Performance and Results Act requires federal agencies to update their strategic plans every 3 years, and EPA is preparing to update its plan. ORD is developing its own updated strategic plan, to be published later this year. It is not expected to change the previously identified high-priority research topics or to depart significantly from the contents of the 1996 plan and 1997 update, but it is expected to add three new high-priority research areas—children's health, safe food, and global change.

Three years after the 1995 reorganization of ORD, its Board of Scientific Counselors (BOSC) expressed concern about the lack of strategic plans at the level of the individual laboratories and centers (EPABOSC 1998a-e). Although ORD had developed an overall strategic plan (EPA 1996a, 1997a), and the ORD national laboratories and centers had each developed mission statements, the BOSC found that none of the laboratories and centers had developed its own strategic plan. Recently, EPA advised our committee that all the laboratories and centers have drafted such plans, but they were developed too late for consideration by the BOSC in its first program reviews, and they were not provided to our committee.

Our committee is not convinced that ORD has provided adequate delegation of opportunities for leadership and accountability throughout the organization. The absence of published strategic and management plans for the laboratories and centers, as noted in the BOSC reviews, is problematic. At a minimum, ORD should make it clear that the directors of the national laboratories, centers, and divisions are responsible for

- Selecting, defining, and justifying the problem priorities for their part of the organization, based upon the overall ORD strategic goals, the comprehensive problem list, and the mission and capabilities of their respective laboratory, center, or division.

- Identifying and developing the research and technical support programs and projects of their laboratory, center, or division, together with an organizational upgrading program that reflects the agreed upon priorities for their part of the organization.
- Effectively executing these programs within the approved budget—a responsibility implying delegated authority to triage various programs within the context of approved budgets and priorities.
- Developing effective channels of communication to ensure timely transfers of information to all levels of the relevant program offices.

The committee also urges that the strategic plans of ORD's laboratories and centers place substantial emphasis on needs and strategies for maintaining and upgrading scientific capabilities, including staff-skill mix, facilities, and equipment.

Strategic planning in ORD has been predominantly a "top-down" and widely inclusive effort, but that is only partially effective. The top-down strategic-planning effort should be matched by and integrated with a "bottom-up" planning approach as research plans are developed pursuant to the strategic plan, especially with regard to specific research program and project proposals. Individual research program and project priorities should be developed by individual laboratories and their divisions in response to the overall strategic goals and missions defined from above. In other words, the mission and goals should largely be defined in a top-down process, but the laboratory programs and projects should be defined in a more bottom-up process by the researchers who will implement them. In the committee's site visits and the BOSC laboratory program reviews, a number of suggestions were heard from principal investigators about the need for the bench and field scientists to have a stronger role in planning the actual research activities in response to the strategic plan. Their well-informed and realistic views of costs, time, probable difficulties, and likely outcomes of research could do much to ensure that ORD's plans are feasible and push the limits of what can be done.

THE ORD LABORATORIES

In the 1995 reorganization, ORD's 12 geographically dispersed laboratories were consolidated into three mega-laboratories, called national laboratories: the National Health and Environmental Effects Research Laboratory, the National Exposure Research Laboratory, and the National Risk Management Research Laboratory.

The National Health and Environmental Effects Research Laboratory (the Effects Laboratory) is the largest ORD laboratory, combining all the former health and ecological research laboratories into one national laboratory with headquarters in Research Triangle Park, NC (see Figure 2-4). In fiscal year 1999 the Effects Laboratory had 708 employees, of which approximately 250 were principal investigators, and its total budget was $118 million, including a $40 million extramural budget. The laboratory is organized into nine divisions; five of them, located in North Carolina and Ohio, address health-effects research—environmental carcinogenesis, experimental toxicology, human studies, reproductive toxicology, and neurotoxicology—and four divisions, located in Florida, Minnesota, Oregon, and Rhode Island, pursue environmental research with, to some extent, a geographical (regional) orientation. As of 1997, approximately 33% of the laboratory's total budget and personnel were in the health divisions, 55% in the environmental divisions, and the remainder in administration (EPABOSC 1998a).

The overall mission of the Effects Laboratory is to perform laboratory and field research to identify and understand the health and ecological effects of environmental stressors and the likelihood of such effects occurring under conditions of environmental exposure. In keeping with ORD's focus on the "risk paradigm," the Effects Laboratory focuses on the first two components of the risk-assessment process, hazard identification and dose-response assessment.

The National Exposure Research Laboratory (the Exposure Laboratory) was formed by combining former ORD laboratories in Research Triangle Park, NC, Cincinnati, OH, Las Vegas, NV, and Athens, GA, with headquarters in Research Triangle Park, NC (see Figure 2-4). In fiscal year 1999, the Exposure Laboratory had 448 employees and a total budget of $109 million, including a $45 million extramural budget. The Exposure Laboratory's overall mission is to perform research and development to characterize, predict, and diagnose exposures to humans and ecosystems, giving priority to the research that most significantly reduces the uncertainty in risk assessment and most improves the tools to assess and manage risk and to characterize compliance with regulations.

The National Risk Management Research laboratory (the Risk Management Laboratory) was formed by combining former ORD laboratories in Cincinnati, OH; Research Triangle Park, NC; Ada, OK; and Washington, DC, with central administration in Cincinnati (see Figure 2-4). In fiscal year 1999, the Risk Management Laboratory had 393 employees and a total budget of $108 million, including a $62 million extramural budget. Of the laboratory's six divisions, four are basically organized according to environmental compartments or media: air, water, land, and subsurface. The other two divisions address sustainable technology and technology transfer.

The Risk Management Laboratory is responsible for developing the scientific basis for environmental risk management affecting both human health and ecosystems. The Risk Management Laboratory conducts research and development on source or problem characterization, prevention methods, control methods, remediation or restoration methods, performance and cost verification, and technology transfer.

In 1996, EPA's ORD requested and obtained under the Federal Advisory Committee Act a charter for a new body, the BOSC, to advise EPA's Assistant Administrator for Research Development. The BOSC is not part of the SAB. Established with 15 senior expert members from universities and other organizations serving on an ongoing basis, including one member of this NRC committee, and augmented with temporary members appointed to serve on ad hoc subcommittees as needed, including additional members of this NRC committee, the BOSC was charged to evaluate the management and operations of ORD's research programs and peer-review practices.

As one of its first tasks, the BOSC was asked to conduct program reviews of the ORD laboratories and centers, including the strategies and practices used by the laboratory and center directors to implement ORD's strategic plan (EPA 1996a, 1997a) and the mission of each laboratory and center. The BOSC accomplished that task through self-study questions and site visits in 1997, and it completed reports of the program reviews in 1998 (EPA BOSC 1998a-e).

The BOSC found much that it liked. Overall, it judged the Effects

Laboratory to be "very solid with a high potential for being a national leader in a number of areas" (EPABOSC 1998a) It concluded that the Effects Laboratory "has a solid research foundation, and has made significant efforts to establish priorities and directions consistent with elements applicable to it in the ORD strategic plan." In the health-effects divisions of the Effects Laboratory, the BOSC especially praised the programs in neurotoxicology, reproductive and developmental toxicology, and human-chamber studies. In the Effects Laboratory's environmental-effects divisions, it praised ecoregions work and landscape ecology at the Corvallis division, freshwater and estuarine toxicity-test methods development at Duluth, and other programs. It commented that staff morale seemed to have improved in the Effects Laboratory since the 1995 reorganization. Principal investigators at the laboratory reported to BOSC that the research environment within the Effects Laboratory had substantially improved in recent years.

The BOSC concluded that the Exposure Laboratory was "conducting some high-quality, peer-reviewed science in high-priority areas for EPA" (EPABOSC 1998b). It noted that the Exposure Laboratory had made significant scientific contributions in source-exposure research; chemical, physical, and biological process modeling, especially urban and regional air-pollution modeling; environmental characterization research; exposure analysis and assessment research; exposure-dose research; analytical measurements; environmental process research; and animal exposure studies.

At the Risk Management Laboratory, the BOSC noted its "excellent national and international reputation for applying sound and innovative engineering principles to identifying and controlling air and water pollutant emissions from a variety of sources" (EPABOSC 1998c). It singled out the Risk Management Laboratory's strong reputation in emission-source characterization, and it credited the laboratory with being "highly responsive to ORD in its attempts to reorient its research planning to conform to the ORD strategic plan."

In addition to the concern noted previously that none of the reorganized laboratories had developed a strategic plan, the BOSC identified other problems. The administrative structure of the Effects Laboratory had not become well established by the time of the BOSC review. The BOSC found that the health-effects research divisions were generally organized by scientific disciplines, but the environmental research divisions were more geographically defined. In addition, the health-effects components of the laboratory had centralized administrative operations, reflecting pre-reorganization practices, while the ecological-effects divisions, each of which had laboratory-level status before the reorganization, retained their own administrative operations. These disparities were reduced somewhat after the BOSC review (Reiter 1999).

At the Exposure Laboratory, the 1995 reorganization of ORD and its immediate aftermath brought a 28% decrease in personnel and a 56% decrease in the laboratory's overall budget. The decreases were due to problems with the conversion of contract personnel to federal positions and major reductions in contract funds (EPABOSC 1998b). These cuts required reductions in technical support for EPA's program offices as the Exposure Laboratory tried to increase its proportional focus on research.

The BOSC concluded that personnel and funding were insufficient to carry out the Exposure Laboratory's mission (EPABOSC 1998b). It expressed concern that only 168 of the 407 staff at the Exposure Laboratory had research degrees at the masters or doctoral level, whereas 103 staff positions were in administrative jobs, and about 45 of those were strictly management. It identified redundant administrative structures at each of the Exposure Laboratory's four locations—Research Triangle Park, NC; Las Vegas, NV; Cincinnati, OH; and Athens, GA. It urged ORD to increase the number of research and technical-support personnel at the Exposure Laboratory and reduce the number of administrators. It urged ORD to emphasize the hiring of postdoctoral researchers and research technicians.

The BOSC also found that ORD's 1995 reorganization plan and 1996-1997 strategic plan had "not infused themselves into the scientific culture" at the Exposure Laboratory. It observed that workers at all levels at the Exposure Laboratory were still trying to understand what the reorganization meant. The BOSC concluded that the reorganization had "not created any scientific excitement among the employees or change in the way they are doing their research." It urged the Exposure Laboratory to maintain its commitment to the ORD reorganization and strategic plan for several years to achieve success.

At the Risk Management Laboratory, the BOSC noted that ORD's 1995 reorganization required the laboratory to broaden its mission considerably while reducing its staff by 70 positions and its extramural resources by 60%, and it expressed concern that the Risk Management Laboratory might not receive the resources minimally needed to fulfill its broadened mission (EPABOSC 1998c). Previously, the Risk Management Laboratory had mainly performed an engineering and technology role, but the laboratory's new risk-management mission posed a considerable challenge and required a fundamental transformation. The BOSC concluded that the available resources and staff of the Risk Management Laboratory were inadequate for its new, broader mission. Such a mission requires resources and expertise in areas such as economics, management science, social and behavioral sciences, microbiology, ecology, systems analysis, and risk communication—resources and expertise that the Risk Management Laboratory lacked. The BOSC expressed concern that such changes might diminish the traditional engineering strengths of the Risk Management Laboratory and noted that the laboratory's longstanding competency in wastewater technology was no longer being used effectively. The BOSC also judged the Risk Management Laboratory's infrastructure to be inadequate. If the necessary resources were not provided to the Risk Management Laboratory, the BOSC recommended that the laboratory's strategic goals and mission be reformulated to be more in line with its staff and facilities. In fact, the BOSC questioned whether ORD had adequately understood the talents and capabilities of the Risk Management Laboratory when it developed its strategic plan.

Noting that the Risk Management Laboratory's research priorities are heavily influenced by statutory requirements or court orders, as well as ORD, the BOSC expressed concern about the vagueness and lack of clarity of the laboratory's understanding of its research scope, how it sets its research priorities, how much flexibility it has in setting such priorities, and how it makes decisions about the allocation of available resources to various research activities. The BOSC also questioned whether the Risk Management Laboratory was preparing adequately to meet the part of its research mission dealing with the management of ecological risks.

Before the 1995 reorganization, as much as 60% of the Risk Management Laboratory's budget had been devoted to outside contracted research; the laboratory's scientific and technical staff were heavily involved in managing extramural projects, and in-house research was minimal (EPABOSC 1998c). When ORD shifted the emphasis from extramural management to in-house research, the shift had a major impact on the Risk Management Laboratory, despite the fact that the Risk Management Laboratory still had 111 active cooperative agreements with 75 academic institutions at the time of the BOSC review (EPABOSC 1998c). The BOSC urged the laboratory to devote high priority to identifying the needed skill mix to perform its broadened mission, acquiring such staff, retraining present staff, and improving the laboratory infrastructure, including laboratory space and equipment. The BOSC also emphasized the need to reduce the burdens of bureaucracy, red tape, unnecessary or redundant committees, and other overhead activities on professional staff (EPABOSC 1998c).

The BOSC emphasized that stability of resources and personnel is critical for maintaining a strong research laboratory (EPABOSC 1998a). It pointed out that regardless of the time frames of EPA's regulatory activities, ORD must operate in a research environment, which requires a stable planning process and longer timetables, and that rapidly shifting priorities and unstable funding are detrimental to a research environment. The BOSC suggested the exploration of ways to improve stability by making resource allocations more flexible.

In addition to the BOSC reviews, each of the ORD national laboratories has conducted its own divisional and programmatic reviews, using experts from outside the agency in a process organized by the laboratory peer-review coordinator (see Chapter 3). The divisional reviews address the scientific content and quality of the activities of each laboratory division. The program reviews focus on the research goals, approaches, progress, and results of large-scale research program areas. Like the BOSC reviews, these divisional and programmatic reviews entailed questions and informational materials prepared in advance, on-site visits, reports for laboratory management, and responses from the laboratory divisions and programs.

Our committee, two members of which participated in the BOSC reviews of the laboratories and centers and most of whom participated in additional site visits to each laboratory and center as described in Chapter 1, generally concurs with the results of the BOSC program reviews. Overall, the committee believes that the 1995 reorganization of the ORD program is still a work in progress, but it has begun to mature, and the committee strongly supports continued efforts to refine it.

During our committee's site visits to the laboratories, we were pleased to meet with many outstanding researchers, some of them with world-class reputations. For example, scientists at the Effects Laboratory, who consistently publish nearly 300 research articles each year in peer-reviewed journals, include the current president of the Society of Environmental Toxicology and Chemistry, the president-elect of the Society of Teratology, and many research scientists who serve on the editorial boards of journals and as adjunct members of the faculties of major universities.

The committee recommends that ORD continue to have its laboratories, laboratory divisions, and major research programs reviewed by panels of outside experts approximately every 5 years. The committee favors having as many of these reviews as possible performed by the BOSC, according to its now-established procedures, because the BOSC has done well in its initial round of reviews, and it advises the assistant administrator for research and development, so it is more independent of laboratory management, or at least perceived to be, than internally managed review groups. However, the committee cautions that excessive use of external review panels can undermine the sense of responsibility of laboratory managers for identifying and resolving problems

Each of the ORD laboratories (and the Assessment Center) has conducted a competitive internal research-grant program. The number of awards and the amounts awarded have been modest, and the programs are being re-evaluated. The committee encourages ORD to pursue them.

THE ORD CENTERS

The 1995 reorganization of ORD created two national centers. The National Center for Environmental Assessment was created from ORD's former Office of Health and Environmental Assessment, including the former Environmental Criteria and Assessment Offices in Cincinnati and Research Triangle Park. The National Center for Environmental Research and Quality Assurance (recently renamed the National Center for Environmental Research) was created from ORD's former headquarters Office of Exploratory Research and charged to implement a greatly expanded research grants and centers program.

In fiscal year 1999, the National Center for Environmental Assessment (the Assessment Center) had 177 employees and a total budget of $35 million, including a $16 million extramural budget. The center develops methodologies for performing risk assessments and reducing the uncertainties in current risk-assessment approaches; conducts assessments of contaminants and sites of national significance; and provides guidance and support to agency risk assessors. It also contributes to the planning of research relevant to those activities.

The National Center for Environmental Research (the Extramural Center) is the smallest of ORD's laboratories and centers in terms of staff. In fiscal year 1999, the center had 90 employees and a total budget of $151 million, $139 million of which was extramural. The Extramural Center is responsible for the programs that fund ORD's extramural research grants, centers, and fellowships. In response to a recommendation from the NRC (1977), ORD has conducted a competitive, peer-reviewed, extramural research-grant program since 1979. Until 1995, funding for the grants program fluctuated between $5 million and $25 million per year.

In *Safeguarding the Future: Credible Science, Credible Decisions* (EPA 1992), an independent panel of senior academic scientists (including two members of our committee) expressed concern that EPA lacked adequate mechanisms for acquiring the best available scientific information from other scientific organizations and the broader scientific community. In 1994, an agency-wide steering committee (EPA 1994b) recommended strengthening the grants program and increasing its size to $100 million a year. It envisioned funding approximately 400 new grants each year, with an average grant lasting 2 or 3 years at an average level of $100,000 per grant year.

Grant funding was dramatically increased in the 1995 reorganization of ORD, and since 1997, the Extramural Center has funded about $100 million per year in its Science to Achieve Results (STAR) program of research grants and fellowships (Figure 2-9). It currently supports about 700 competitively awarded research grants, 15 research centers, and 300 EPA fellowships each year, all awarded through national competition (Figure 2-10). Each year it receives about 3,000 to 3,500 proposals and awards about 200 new grants and 120 new graduate fellowships. The Extramural Center's programs are administered by two divisions, one devoted to environmental science and the other to environmental engineering.

There were two primary reasons why EPA decided to strengthen

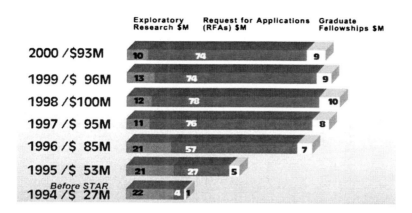

FIGURE 2-9   STAR Program by components, 1994–2000. Source: EPA.

and expand the extramural research-grant program. First, recognizing that the immense need for scientific and technical knowledge about environmental problems far exceeded any realistic assessment of the budgets and capabilities of EPA's in-house laboratories, the agency wanted to increase greatly the collaboration and potential contributions of the nation's academic community through an expanded and strengthened, competitive, investigator-initiated grants program. Second, as discussed in the next section of this chapter, the agency wanted to reverse the trend of previous years in which many in-house research scientists and engineers in ORD laboratories were increasingly spending their time as administrators of extramurally funded projects at the cost of doing less and less in-house research. The primary concern was that EPA's laboratories were losing their expertise and abilities to perform first-rate research. In addition, concerns were heard about favoritism and poor oversight in the administration of some externally funded projects by EPA laboratory personnel. To change that, the agency centralized much of its extramural research funding in a rigorously competitive STAR grants program, and it sent a strong message to in-house laboratory staff that they would be expected to do more research

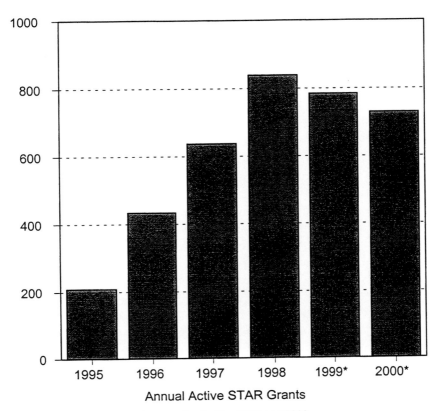

Annual Active STAR Grants

*Number of awards are estimated for 1999 and 2000.

FIGURE 2-10 Active STAR research grants by year. Source: EPA.

and less administration, and that they would be judged mainly by research accomplishments in the future.

Topics for STAR program solicitations are developed in a process that begins with agency-wide research-coordination teams that include representatives from ORD's national laboratories and centers, as well as EPA regulatory and regional offices. After considering the ORD strategic plan, the needs of other EPA offices, and input from external groups, decisions about potential solicitation topics are made on the basis of such criteria as the need for improving risk assessment or risk management in a topic area, the suitability of the topic for the grants process, the extent to which the topic may complement or be performed instead by in-house research programs, the possibility of collaborative funding with other federal agencies, and the availability of resources. The proposed solicitation topics are reviewed by ORD's Science Council and Executive Council. Solicitation topics of potential interest to other agencies are considered in interagency discussions and by the Committee on Environment and Natural Resources of the National Science and Technology Council.

Peer review, discussed in detail in the next chapter of this report, is a major activity and defining feature of the Extramural Center. EPA's longstanding regulations (40 CFR Part 40 Section 40.150) for peer review of research grants and cooperative agreements specify that new grant applications "will be reviewed for technical merit by at least one reviewer within EPA and at least two reviewers outside EPA." The regulations also specify review by EPA staff for other criteria, such as relevancy to EPA's needs and priorities. In 1995, at the direction of Congress, ORD began awarding a substantial portion of its grants through a process conducted jointly with the National Science Foundation (NSF). Working in partnership, ORD and NSF developed joint program announcements, peer-review procedures, and funding for several areas of research solicitations of mutual interest.

Today, peer reviews for scientific merit in the EPA STAR grants program are conducted under policies and practices that are generally modeled after those of NSF (1998) and are also similar in many ways to the extramural grants programs of the National Institutes of Health (NIH) (42 CFR Part 52h). All three agencies use external expert reviewers to assess the scientific and technical merit of extramural research proposals in a competitive award process.

The EPA STAR program, with a budget of $96 million in fiscal year 1999, receives approximately 3,000 to 3,500 applications per year for research grants, centers, and fellowships, demonstrating considerable interest from the academic community. In each of the past few years, roughly 20% of these applications have been judged through peer review as meritorious for potential funding, and about half of the meritorious applications have received funding (i.e., approximately 10% of the applications received). In fiscal year 1998, the latest year for which complete data are available, the STAR program received 1,666 research-grant applications, judged 389 of them to merit funding, and awarded funding for 167; an additional 37 grants were funded by other federal agencies participating with EPA in the solicitations. In the same year, the STAR program received 1,251 fellowship applications, judged 168 of them to be excellent, and awarded 126.

NSF, with a much larger research-grant budget of about $2.5 billion out of its $3.9 billion total agency budget, reviews about 30,000 proposals each year and funds about 10,000 new awards annually, funding approximately 27% of the proposals it receives. NIH, with an even larger budget of about $17.9 billion in fiscal year 2000, reviews about 40,000 grant applications annually through its Center for Scientific Review and funds about 30%. The EPA STAR grants are typically funded for up to 3 years, although there are exceptions. The NSF grants are commonly funded for 1 to 5 years. NIH restricts funding of new grants to 25% of its grants budget to ensure continued funding for ongoing grants.

One important difference between the EPA grants program and the NSF and NIH programs in terms of peer-review practices derives from the different agency missions. NSF and NIH are science agencies, so their reviews focus mainly on technical merit and potential impacts of the proposed research. EPA, with its environmental protection mission, subjects research proposals to separate reviews for technical merit and relevance to the agency's program needs. The relevancy review is performed on applications rated meritorious by the merit-review panels. EPA program offices are consulted, often through research coordination teams, in the relevancy reviews. The relevancy reviews focus on criteria such as relevance to ORD's overall research strategy, potential to reduce scientific, risk-related uncertainties in decision-making, and applicability to agency programs and priorities.

In the EPA grants process, the merit reviews are performed by panels of outside experts, mostly from the academic community, in a process organized and led by a science review administrator on the staff of the ORD Extramural Center. The Extramural Center maintains a computerized Peer Review Panelist Information System containing resumes and other information about potential reviewers to support this process. Typically, each research application is submitted to three principal reviewers, and each reviewer is assigned approximately eight applications. The reviewers are consulted in decisions about the applications to be assigned to them. They generally serve under a professional services contract. Each reviewer receives the applications at least 4 weeks before the panel meeting, as well as information about the solicitation to which the applications are responding, the review process and criteria, the conflict-of-interest guidelines, the other applications being reviewed by other experts on the panel, and other materials. Each reviewer prepares a written evaluation of each assigned application and gives it an overall rating. In the panel meeting, the applications are sorted into two groups: those having the greatest merit and those having lesser merit. All applications in the first group are presented by the panelists who reviewed them and discussed by the full panel. The panel then rates them by vote. Anonymous summaries of panel evaluations and, if requested, anonymous evaluations are provided to applicants.

In a generally similar process, NSF grant proposals are reviewed by an NSF program officer plus several external experts chosen by the program officer. NIH grant proposals are reviewed by a grants referral officer and then by a scientific review group, typically about 20 active biomedical researchers, mostly from outside NIH. They are appointed to multiyear terms upon the recommendation of a scientific review administrator and meet or teleconference about three times a year, sometimes seeking additional outside opinions.

Merit review criteria in the EPA grants program address both the research proposal and the investigator. For the proposal, reviewers are asked to assess factors such as originality, creativity, potential scientific knowledge contributions, appropriateness and adequacy of methods, technical merit of the proposed approach, feasibility, and quality assurance plans. For the investigator, reviewers are asked to evaluate qualifications, demonstrated knowledge, publication record, and time commitment. In a similar process, merit review criteria in NSF emphasize the intellectual merit of proposed research and its potential contributions to education and other societal goals. Also similarly, NIH criteria emphasize the potential significance of proposed research, the proposed approach, innovation, the qualifications of investigators, and the research environment. EPA, NSF, and NIH also consider inclusion and recruitment of minorities and the protection of humans, animals, and the environment.

All EPA research grantees are required to provide annual and final progress reports. ORD's Extramural Center posts abstracts of these reports on its web site. The center's web site also contains all grant solicitations, lists all funded grants and centers, and provides a keyword search function. The center conducts annual all-investigator meetings for individual solicitation categories and prepares special summary reports of results and research-in-progress reports in selected topic areas. The center seeks to involve ORD laboratory personnel and promote communication with regulatory program staff in the grants program through its web site, special reports, progress-review workshops, and other mechanisms, including informal communication.

In 1997-1998, ORD's BOSC conducted program reviews of the national centers, as they also did for the national laboratories (see previous section). Reviewers included 15 senior expert members from universities and other organizations serving on an ongoing basis, including one member of our committee, and augmented with temporary members appointed to serve on ad hoc subcommittees as needed, including additional members of our committee. The BOSC focused on the mission of each center and the strategies and practices used by the center directors to implement ORD's strategic plan (EPA 1996a, 1997a). As with the national laboratories, the BOSC accomplished the review through self-study questions and site visits in 1997 and completed reports of the program reviews in 1998 (EPABOSC 1998d-e).

As with the national laboratories, the BOSC found positive things to say about the centers. It judged the mission of the Assessment Center to be of "significant value to ORD if attained" and observed "many positive attributes and strengths" within the Assessment Center, including "high quality and productivity of its scientific expertise" (EPABOSC 1998d).

The BOSC had high praise for the Extramural Center, commenting that "Center management and staff have exhibited extraordinary creativity and hard work in initiating programs to accomplish [the center's] mission" (EPABOSC 1998e). It applauded the "quality and commitment" of the center's director and staff as "quite impressive." It particularly commended the Extramural Center's efforts to improve the integration of research efforts and the communication of results to target audiences. It praised the center's joint solicitations with other agencies and organizations; Adopt-a-Grant program for ORD laboratory scientists; workshop, research-in-progress, and state-of-the-science reports; web site; and other efforts to communicate program results to other EPA offices and outside audiences.

As with the national laboratories, the BOSC found that neither of the national centers, created in 1995, had yet developed its own strategic plan (EPABOSC 1998d,e).

The BOSC judged that too much of the Assessment Center's effort was being devoted to high-profile issues, short-term problems, and "firefighting," and the Assessment Center was often stretched too thin (EPABOSC 1998d). In view of the agency's vast needs for risk assessments, the many risk-assessment activities being performed by the agency's regulatory program offices, and the limited resources available to the Assessment Center, the BOSC urged the Assessment Center to rethink its role and become more of a risk-assessment leader, catalyst, and resource service center for the other offices of the agency—a source of advice, guidance, and methodology—rather than a primary performer of individual risk assessments. The BOSC suggested that the Assessment Center could be most effective by focusing not on performing or trying to "own" or control individual risk assessments, but rather on improving and supporting the scientific underpinnings of the risk assessments performed across the agency through the development, acquisition, testing, and maintenance of state-of-the-art methods and information that support the agency's risk-assessment activities. The BOSC urged the Assessment Center to promote the suggested role by working creatively and aggressively to strengthen its relationships with other agency programs and understand their needs and expectations for risk-assessment services. The BOSC also suggested that the Assessment Center strengthen its relationships with ORD's national laboratories and ORD-supported academic research centers to promote research relevant to the Assessment Center's mission.

The BOSC expressed concern about the adequacy of the size and skill mix of the Extramural Center's limited staff resources in view of the enormous recent growth of the grants program, which had not been accompanied by commensurate growth in staff size or other internal resources (EPABOSC 1998e). The BOSC was concerned about the ability of the Extramural Center's staff to manage effectively the administrative and technical aspects of the greatly expanded program. In particular, the BOSC was concerned about the growing workloads and skill mix of the center's project officers. It expressed concerns about the adequacy of time and resources to track progress on awarded grants, facilitate appropriate interactions with and among researchers, and ensure that the results of grantees' research are communicated to the rest of the agency and other interested groups. The BOSC recommended greater streamlining of grant and fellowship management practices and greater prioritization of the target audiences for the communication of research results.

The BOSC also raised questions about the Extramural Center's funding for social-science research. EPA support for social-science research has largely been limited to economic topics such as resource valuation or regulatory compliance costs. The BOSC noted the dearth of social scientists other than economists in EPA and wondered how the Extramural Center would be able to deal with such research areas as human behavior, risk perception and communication, law, history, philosophy, and ethics. It suggested that the Extramural Center seek help from other agencies with more experience in these areas.

Our committee generally concurs with the BOSC assessments of the national centers (EPABOSC 1998d,e). It is clear that the Assessment Center performs an important service to the agency in its methodological development work and other activities, including its support of the agency-wide Risk Assessment Forum. We also note that the Assessment Center has often made good use of outside expert advice. For example, in its development of agency risk-assessment guidelines, the Assessment Center has been highly responsive to many of the recommendations of the National Research Council's 1994 report *Science and Judgment in Risk Assessment* (NRC 1994c). Our committee especially concurs with the BOSC recommendation that the Assessment Center focus on being an advisor, catalyst, and resource for risk assessments conducted by the rest of the agency, rather than trying to do many risk assessments with its own limited resources. The Assessment Center should focus on being a research organization dedicated to advancing the state of practice in risk assessment, not a performer of individual risk assessments that could be done by EPA's regulatory offices.

We commend the Extramural Center for developing and conducting the STAR research-grants program in an open, careful, and credible process of national competition and independent merit review. This program has become a valuable mechanism by which EPA engages outside scientific and engineering talent in the agency's research program. Our committee further believes that the Extramural Center merits strong praise for the steps it has taken to collaborate with other funding agencies and organizations, including joint research-grant solicitations with

- the National Science Foundation, on water and watersheds, technology for a sustainable environment, decision-making and valuation for environmental policy, and environmental statistics;
- the National Institute of Environmental Health Sciences, on children's environmental health and disease prevention, chemical mixtures in environmental health, and endocrine disruptors;
- other components of the National Institutes of Health on genetic susceptibility and human malformations;
- the National Aeronautics and Space Administration, on ecosystem restoration, hazardous algal blooms, and ecological effects of environmental stressors using coastal intensive sites;
- the National Oceanic and Atmospheric Administration, on ecological effects of environmental stressors using coastal intensive sites;
- the Department of Energy, on bioremediation; and
- the Office of Naval Research, on bioremediation.

At a smaller level, the Extramural Center has collaborated in grants solicitations with the American Water Works Association Research Foundation, the Association of California Water Authorities, and the Chemical Manufacturers Association.

EPA can derive substantial benefits from these joint solicitation programs. They enable the participating agencies and organizations to learn from each other, pool and leverage resources, engage experts who normally work with other agencies, and expand the scope and use of the research results to more stakeholder audiences and users. These are win-win ventures.

The committee also commends the Extramural Center for developing and maintaining its excellent internet site, which makes available to everyone the abstracts of research applications funded by the Extramural Center and its interagency partners, the annual and final reports from grantees, and reports of workshops on the integration of research results and their relevance for decision-making.

The committee encourages the Extramural Center to continue its development of state-of-the-science reports on topics of grant solicitations. Such reports can be of considerable value in communicating to others the results of research funded by the Extramural Center and its interagency partners, current knowledge in a given area, policy implications of what is known, and gaps in knowledge that can guide future research.

Although the committee supports the strengthened and expanded STAR grants program, it also recognizes that the funds used to increase the program approximately fourfold, from $23 million in 1993 to approximately $100 million today, came from reductions in other ORD programs. Much of it came from funds that the laboratories had previously used for interagency agreements, cooperative agreements, and contracts with other research organizations in government, the academic community, and the private sector. In its site visits to the laboratories, the members of this committee heard concerns from some ORD managers and staff about what they perceived to be the "loss" of these funds, and they lamented the damaging effects of the change on their laboratories' relationships with the outside research community.

The committee strongly supports the Extramural Center's undergraduate and graduate fellowship programs, as discussed in the next section of this chapter, and commends the agency for establishing them.

The committee recommends that ORD continue to have both of its national centers, and major programs within them, reviewed by panels of outside experts approximately every 5 years. The committee favors having as many of these reviews as possible performed by the BOSC, according to its now-established procedures because the BOSC has done well in its initial round of reviews, and it advises the assistant administrator for research and development, so it is more independent of center management, or at least perceived to be, than internally managed review groups.

THE SCIENTIFIC WORK FORCE

For ORD and other offices of EPA, the ability to attract, retain, and support a capable and dedicated work force of scientists, engineers, technicians, managers, other professionals, and support staff is the most critical requirement for strong scientific and technical performance. Our committee is aware of many excellent scientists and engineers in ORD who are highly qualified; perform first-rate research; publish in peer-reviewed journals; and participate actively in professional societies, advisory panels, and university faculties. The committee's site visits to ORD laboratories and centers were especially encouraging in that regard, and the committee strongly concurs with the judgments expressed by ORD's BOSC (EPABOSC 1998a-e) concerning the substantial number of highly capable and productive staff members in the ORD laboratories and centers. Yet, the maintenance and proper support of a first-rate scientific and technical work force have always posed difficult challenges for EPA.

The ORD work force is aging. More than 47% of ORD's employees are 50 years old or older, and more than 550 ORD employees will be eligible to retire within the next 5 years. Periodic EPA hiring freezes, combined with intense scientific and technical job-market competition from the private sector and academic institutions, are making it extremely difficult for ORD to recruit the new talent needed to sustain and enhance its research work force.

Safeguarding the Future: Credible Science, Credible Decisions (EPA 1992) concluded that an inadequate infrastructure and lack of long-term support have limited EPA's ability to attract and retain outstanding scientists, and that EPA did not yet have the critical mass of such scientists needed to make EPA science generally credible to the broader scientific community. The 1992 report recommended continued attention to appropriate science and science-management career tracks—research career tracks for scientists in ORD, and career tracks for scientists in the agency's program and regional offices that are similar to those for agency attorneys. It emphasized that the criteria for scientific promotion in EPA should include evidence of continuing advancement in a scientific discipline, such as completion of coursework, receipt of board certification, publications in the scientific literature, and contributions to the work of scientific organizations. The report recommended that a panel of scientists from universities and other agencies regularly evaluate the productivity of EPA scientists as a requirement for promotion within the agency. It urged that compensation for EPA scientists be based on competition with the best of their peers. It emphasized the need to minimize the bureaucratic duties of scientists and to ensure that they spend a significant percentage of their time on scientific activities. The report also recommended increased contact and enhanced rotational opportunities to enable EPA scientists to participate in the broader scientific community, including participation in academic organizations, professional society activities, industry, and other federal agencies. It also recommended rotational opportunities for non-EPA scientists to work in EPA science programs.

The 1992 report recommended that ORD recruit and make a long-term commitment of support for four to six research scientists and engineers with world-class reputations in areas vital to EPA's long-term strategy and direction. The panel envisioned that these eminent scientists and engineers would serve as examples and mentors for all scientists in EPA and would bring access to networks of world-class scientists to benefit the agency. The panel recommended that EPA's Science Advisory Board be asked to form a search committee.

In a self-study report prepared for ORD's BOSC, the Effects Laboratory identified expanded appointment authority to attract and retain high-quality professionals as one of its greatest needs (EPABOSC 1998a). It expressed concern about its ability to compete with industry and academia in some areas. The Effects Laboratory expressed support for ORD's postdoctoral program and suggested the creation of a mechanism similar to the Senior Scientific Leadership Corps created by Congress for the Department of Health and Human Services.

Because of rapid scientific advances, EPA has a continuing need to reassess its research skill base and increase its scientific and engineering capabilities in many areas, such as epidemiology, molecular toxicology, and industrial ecology. Economics and the social sciences are also of critical importance to EPA, especially in cost-benefit analysis and other decision-making aids. During the 1970s and early 1980s, ORD had an active in-house program of economic and social-science research, including both methodological development and applied studies. In 1983, this program and the resources supporting it were transferred to EPA's policy office; the budget for that program diminished considerably and was recently eliminated. ORD has continued to fund extramural economic and social science research at a modest level through its competitive grants program, and the policy office and EPA regulatory offices perform some economic studies, but EPA's in-house program in economics and social-science research has diminished from approximately 30 ORD staff members in the 1970s to an almost entirely grants-based extramural program today. During the

1980s, EPA's policy office performed an economics oversight role for the agency through its regulatory impact-analysis function, but that role has since diminished.

ORD's graduate and postdoctoral fellowship programs have become an outstanding asset to the agency. This program is helping to develop the next generation of environmental scientists and provides valuable new talent to ORD's national laboratories. To prevent future shortages of environmental science and engineering personnel in critical disciplines, the federal investment in education programs should generally keep pace with overall research and development needs. Thus, EPA's fellowship program should emphasize specialities for which there is evidence of strong current and future demands. For example, in certain areas of specialization in toxicology, the current disparity between supply and demand is acute. Neurotoxicologists and genetic toxicologists who work on environmental problems are in short supply. The availability of social scientists adequately prepared for environmental research is also severely limited. EPA's fellowships program should emphasize disciplines such as these.

The committee recognizes that estimation of future research work force needs and projected resources can be difficult in disciplines related to environmental protection and environmental health. Estimates can be made, however. Trends in job placements, the number of people completing educational requirements in individual disciplines, and the public and private funding for environmental programs should be among the factors in determining the scope, emphasis, and priority specialization areas for educational support through EPA's graduate-student fellowship program.

In its 1995 reorganization, ORD sought to reverse the trend of previous years in which many in-house research scientists and engineers in ORD laboratories were increasingly spending their time as administrators of extramurally funded projects at the cost of doing less and less in-house research. The primary concern was that EPA's laboratories were losing their expertise and abilities to perform first-rate research.

As one ORD employee put it (Budde 1997),

> *In the early days of federal environmental research at EPA, government research scientists and engineers worked with their technicians in laboratories and pilot plants. It was hands-on R&D, and these people had the respect of their scientific colleagues in academia and industry.*

As Congress passed one after another piece of environmental legislation, with daunting requirements and timetables, it provided EPA with ever-growing quantities of extramural research money instead of authorization to hire more federal scientists and engineers.

EPA research scientists and engineers were offered promotions, power, and influence by becoming administrators of money instead of leaders of science and engineering. The few new hires were almost always managers or administrative support people. Gradually over the past 15 or more years, most EPA research scientists and engineers became money managers and administrators. EPA research by its own federal staff was ignored and even discouraged by management, and so it was effectively destroyed except in a few isolated pockets. Spending the big extramural bucks received all the attention.

In addition, concerns were heard about favoritism and poor oversight by ORD laboratory personnel in the administration of some externally funded projects. To change that, the agency centralized much of its extramural research funding in a rigorously competitive STAR grants program, and it sent a strong message to in-house laboratory staff that they would be expected to do more research and less administration, and that they would be judged mainly by research accomplishments in the future.

One of the nine strategic principles established by ORD states, "Through an innovative and effective human resources development program, nurture and support the development of outstanding scientists, engineers, and other environmental professionals at EPA." In a 1996 workshop involving a cross-section of staff from ORD's laboratories, centers, and offices (EPA 1997a), participants identified the following general work-force-support needs to be of the highest priority:

- *Reduce red tape — Empower staff by reducing unnecessary paperwork.*
- *Communications — Develop and implement a comprehensive communications plan to improve two-way communication and make electronic communications more effective within ORD.*
- *Career advancement and development — Provide career enhancement opportunities for all employees.*
- *Resources and infrastructure — Define "infrastructure" and provide adequate resources to support science.*

To address those issues and others, ORD established a Human Resources Council in 1996. Chaired by an ORD laboratory director, the council has 25 members representing staff from each ORD office, center, and laboratory, with at least one representative from each geographical location, as well as representatives from the agency's human resources office, labor unions, and civil rights office.

One of the most important goals of the Human Resources Council should be to help managers within ORD identify ways to improve and maintain staff morale. Achieving and maintaining good morale are essential to EPA, whose future is inevitably affected by the zeal and confidence with which the staff carries out its work. Good morale is difficult if not impossible to define, however. It might be observed through the pride of employees in being identified with the agency and their pleasure in working for it, but perhaps the most obvious way to recognize morale, like health, is when it is damaged. Staff morale is a fragile thing, and motivational systems that are improperly devised or administered can damage it.

The committee was pleased to observe in its laboratory site visits that ORD has many competent and dedicated scientists, engineers, and other staff. At times, however, many ORD staff have been discouraged and pessimistic about the future of ORD and frustrated and uncertain about prospects for their own professional careers within ORD. The concerns heard by our committee were many: too much disruptive change in budgets, priorities, and policies, often crisis-driven; excessively bureaucratic procedural hurdles; too many scientifically underqualified administrators instead of research scientists managing laboratory programs; failure to replace departing scientists and technicians with new talent in a timely manner; lack of trust up and down the management chain; institutional faultfinding and paranoia; inadequate travel funds and other infrastructure support for nonmanagerial scientists; lack of explanations for decisions; unkept promises; criticism from Congress and others; pessimism that anyone will listen or be able to help. Undoubtedly, some of these complaints reflected individual problems, and ORD management has taken steps to address some of them. But feedback is a valuable commodity, and it pays to keep listening.

The committee offers the following observations and recommendations for developing and supporting the scientific work force.

Continuity

Over EPA's 30-year history, the priorities, initiatives, and operating policies of ORD have often changed sporadically in response to shifting agency demands, the goals and priorities of different administrations, and congressional mandates. Although the much-decried "pollutant-of-the-week" syndrome might be an overstatement, "priority-of-the-year" is close enough to the truth to be of concern in a research program. The sporadic character of research funding for major air pollutants is an example (Powell 1999). Too often, research on a particular pollutant becomes a high priority a year or two before a National Ambient Air Quality Standard is to be evaluated—usually too late for long-term studies. Then, after the agency has made a decision, administrative interest wanes and work is curtailed, despite the certainty, embodied in the Clean Air Act requirement for a re-evaluation every 5 years, that another cycle of interest will soon begin.

Research programs require the development of scientific and engineering talent, experience, and infrastructure. They cannot be turned off and on rapidly. Research requires a longer time scale than nonscientists often appreciate. A lack of stability in goals, priorities, practices, structure, or funding can be especially harmful to a research organization. ORD's historical lack of stability and sometimes disruptive changes have been attributed to growth in EPA's legislative mandates and priorities; specific directives from Congress in the appropriations process; changes in political administrations; changes in public attitudes; lawsuits and court decisions affecting regulatory programs and associated scientific needs; pressures from public groups or regulated parties; inadequate budgets to meet competing demands; recommendations from outside groups; and changes in the leadership of ORD.

The limited financial and human resources of ORD should be managed with a steady hand and a clear and persistent vision of how to maximize the gains in scientific understanding from ORD's budget and the creative time and energy of its staff. ORD should try to refrain from making abrupt shifts in research priorities or internal processes. It should seek feedback and consultation from staff at all levels and provide timely fore-warning when changes will be needed regarding in-house or extramural research budgets, responsibilities, organizational structure, or priorities for research projects, programs, and funding mechanisms.

Bureaucracy

ORD and EPA should make a special effort to resist a tendency commonly seen in large institutions to impose cumbersome bureaucratic procedures in response to management concerns. Institutional paranoia, fault-finding, and fear of possible fault-finding can paralyze and demoralize an organization. Excessively bureaucratic procedures are antithetical to a creative research program with high standards of quality, efficiency, and teamwork. ORD should frequently examine itself to identify and eliminate excessive bureaucratic safeguards, administrative hurdles, redundant requirements for approvals at multiple levels of management, and other bureaucratic impediments.

Research leaders at all levels in ORD should strive to minimize bureaucratic impediments, provide timely responses to requests from other organizations and from staff scientists and engineers, and place high priority on finding ways to increase flexibility in getting research done. ORD managers throughout the organization should be given the authority and resources to make decisions at the lowest appropriate level of management, provided that such decisions are compatible with EPA policies and ORD's strategic goals and budget priorities. Decisions that fit within this category include problem selection and program definition; acquisition of most equipment and supplies, personnel assignment; attendance at scientific meetings; inviting and supporting a visiting scientist; and granting permission for ORD scientists to work for a time in another laboratory in this country or abroad.

Staff Development

An organization that does not adequately aid the continuing improvement of its employees is remiss in its responsibilities and in the long run handicaps itself. Continuing career development for ORD's research staff is critical to the quality and productivity of their research. Opportunities for professional development are especially important for ORD scientists and engineers who, in the 1995 reorganization of ORD discussed earlier in this chapter, were asked to return to research after functioning as managers of extramurally funded projects.

In addition to in-service training, career development includes participation in professional society meetings and activities, as well as collaboration with scientists in other federal agencies, research centers, and universities. The Individual Development Plan (IDP) seems to receive wide support in ORD. The IDP is negotiated between each employee and supervisor. It addresses career paths, training, and rotational goals. The committee also recommends that ORD expand its programs for intellectual growth and exchange with other research organizations. Additional resources are needed for travel to scientific meetings and collaboration with scientists in distant laboratories inside and outside EPA. There is widespread dissatisfaction among ORD research staff with the lack of travel support to enable such interactions. The lack of such support inhibits their ability to share their results with the scientific community at large through participation in conferences and workshops and to develop and sustain meaningful scientific collaborations with scientists at other institutions.

Mentoring of junior staff—scientific and support staff alike—is another key element of a successful research program. The committee observed many elements of a mentoring program in ORD's laboratories. The committee recommends that ORD establish a more formal mentoring program to promote professional growth of all of its junior staff.

The committee recommends that ORD increase sabbatical assignments for ORD researchers to gain experience in other scientific organizations, and that ORD bring more scientists from universities, other government agencies, and private organizations to ORD laboratories and centers for visiting appointments.

Recruitment

The long-term success of EPA's research and development program depends on a staff of well-trained, creative scientists, engineers, and other professionals. Personnel policies affecting the recruitment, retention, and support of research personnel at ORD are critical. ORD often has not provided recruitment and retention packages for research scientists and engineers that are competitive with those of other research organizations in academe or industry. While federal personnel policies impose limits and difficulties, the difficulties can be overcome, as demonstrated by the strong in-house research programs of NIH and NIST. In 1989, ORD instituted a new program for the recruitment and promotion of a limited number of nonmanagerial, senior scientific and technical research and development staff at its laboratories and centers. ORD currently has eight scientists and engineers serving in such positions, which are called "ST" positions. Individuals in those positions are paid at Senior Executive Service levels, and recruitment bonuses up to 25% of annual salary are allowable. No managerial duties are required in these research positions. ORD instituted a special board and has additional experts on an ad hoc basis to review the scientific and technical qualifications of both in-house and external candidates and the performance of individuals in such positions. The board includes senior staff from the ORD laboratories and centers, as well as outside scientists and engineers who are typically at the level of full professor. In fiscal year 1999, ORD promoted four in-house research scientists to ST positions.

EPA has also established an excellent fellowships program, which is intended to revitalize the ORD work force through an infusion of young scientists and engineers. Fellows are selected through a merit-based, competitive process in targeted scientific and technical disciplines relevant to needs identified by ORD. They are generally appointed for 3-year terms, with salaries ranging from about $40,000 to $60,000 per year, full employee benefits, and relocation expenses. ORD advertises the program through professional scientific societies, university graduate departments, scientific periodicals, and EPA's web site. In fiscal year 1999, ORD sought candidates in water resources engineering and management; urban and regional planning; environmental science; chemistry; biology (e.g., cell, developmental, molecular, reproductive, neurobiology, and animal and plant physiology); biochemistry; physical chemistry; human health sciences; endocrinology; epidemiology; pharmacology; toxicology, population and community modeling; geography; microbiology; hydrology; ecology (e.g., aquatic, coastal systems, coral, ecosystem, estuarine, landscape, marine, and microbial); ecotoxicology; meteorology; applied mathematics and statistics; systems analysis; computer science; geographic information science; geomorphology; geostatistics; genetics; immunology; environmental, chemical, and biomedical engineering; and other disciplines. In the first year of the program, ORD was swamped with nearly 2,500 applications for 100 available fellowships. In 1999, ORD received 1,061 applications for 50 available positions. ORD placed 47 applicants in the laboratories, including 15 at the Effects Laboratory, 21 at the Exposure Laboratory, and 11 at the Risk Management Laboratory; and 3 went to ORD's Assessment Center. The 50 included 28 women and 10 minority fellows. In fiscal year 2000, ORD received 798 applications but was only able to hire 16 candidates due to an agency hiring freeze.

Leadership

Criteria for the selection and advancement of research managers in ORD should emphasize persons who are accomplished scientists in their own right and have the ability to select, inspire, lead, and otherwise encourage other scientists and engineers to succeed in meeting agency research needs by pushing back the frontiers of understanding in their fields of special competence.

The following criteria are suggested:

- Accomplishments in original scientific research, demonstrated by publication in refereed scientific or engineering journals.
- Demonstrated ability to develop and implement high quality scientific and engineering research projects and programs relevant to agency and national needs.
- Credibility and reputation in the scientific community.
- Ability to select, inspire, and lead scientists and engineers to further their professional development by increasing their scientific and technical competence and their ability to summarize and add to the policy-relevant scientific and engineering knowledge needed by EPA and the nation.
- Ability to communicate research needs, plans, and results to policy-makers, Congress, the scientific community, stakeholder groups, and the public.

Research managers in ORD should be scientifically and technically accomplished, but they should also be capable administrators and personnel managers. The selection of capable people, their support and development, and sometimes their discharge are among the most important tasks any ORD supervisor should perform. Failure to take the time to choose wisely in the first place or to work as long and as patiently as it takes to help a miscast employee move into a better role within the research program, or out of the office altogether, can result in more lost time and declining public support than virtually any other mistakes. Leaders in ORD should consult regularly with, and be perceived to seek and consider advice from, the scientists and engineers within ORD. Research managers in ORD should be selected on the basis of scientific competence and the personnel skills needed to lead and nurture professional development of their staff scientists and engineers.

Our committee's vision for the future of EPA's research program requires leaders who have technical competence; managerial abilities; communication skills; knowledge and skills in research planning and administration and in the public decision process, including its political dimensions; and the ability to marshal constituencies for an effective research program.

The issue of scientific leadership is discussed further in the last chapter of this report.

3

Peer-Review Practices at EPA

PURPOSES AND BENEFITS OF PEER REVIEW

PEER review is a widely used, time-honored practice in the scientific and engineering community for judging and potentially improving a scientific or technical plan, proposal, activity, program, or work product through documented critical evaluation by individuals or groups with relevant expertise who had no involvement in developing the object under review (see Lock 1985; Rennie 1990; Rennie and Flanagin 1994, 1998; NRC 1998b). Peer review seeks to assess and potentially to foster the improvement of scientific and technical methodology, evidence, criteria, assumptions, calculations, extrapolations, inferences, interpretations, and documentation.

When scientific and technical information is used as part of the basis for a public-policy decision, peer review can substantially enhance not only the quality but also the credibility of the scientific or technical basis for the decision. After-the-fact criticisms of the science are more difficult to sustain if it can be shown to have been properly and independently peer reviewed.

In addition to benefitting the end-products of scientific work, peer review of the plans or early stages of a technical effort can promote efficiency by helping to steer further work in productive directions.

Peer review is not monolithic. There are considerable differences

99

among the logic, social dynamics, procedures, and validity of various forms of peer review. For example, peer review of a prospective (planning) document is typically more tentative than review of a final work product. Similarly, peer reviews of broad programs are different from reviews of individual reports.

LIMITATIONS OF PEER REVIEW

Peer review is not quality assurance or quality control per se. It is essentially advisory, not controlling. Although it can be an important guide and aid to those responsible for ensuring quality, the essence of peer review is to criticize constructively, not to decide. Peer review relies on impartial, independent experts who might have expertise only on some portion of the scope of the work and typically have many other demands competing for their time. The experts performing reviews cannot be expected to be aware of all scientific areas, practical considerations, or constraints of the subject of review, nor should they be held responsible for the ultimate decisions beyond their own review comments. They cannot be held responsible for matters beyond their expertise or, ultimately, for the quality of a work product they did not produce. Those decisions should reside with the individuals and organizations responsible for the outcome. A decision-maker needs to know the views of qualified peers, but such peers often cannot be expected to integrate factors outside the document presented for review, such as the relevance, need, and priority of a new research activity or the role of research findings in a context that necessarily includes statutory requirements, economics, and many other considerations.

The value of the peer-review process in assessing and improving a scientific or technical work product depends on a strong commitment to conduct and apply the results of peer review appropriately in judging or improving the technical merit of the product. The benefits of peer review are diminished if the integrity of the peer-review process is compromised or if the criticisms and suggestions received from independent peer reviewers are to some degree ignored or taken lightly by decision-makers who may be more interested in meeting a deadline or producing a desired answer than in judging or enhancing technical merit.

Peer review is an expensive and personnel-intensive process. It requires the services of many types of persons — skilled program officers and advisers, imaginative investigators, competent peer reviewers, and efficient grants-administration specialists. These individuals should work together in a constructive, trusting, and harmonious way to make the peer-review process effective and efficient. It is also very important that the limited supply of qualified peer reviewers be utilized efficiently. The cost of a peer review effort should be carefully considered in terms of in-house staff time and resources, as well as the limited time and energy of busy experts who must take time from other worthwhile endeavors.

Excessive application of peer review in some cases (e.g., laboratory program reviews) can be disruptive to a research organization and might diminish the sense of responsibility of laboratory managers to take appropriate measures on their own.

Peer review cannot substitute for technically competent work in the development of a product. It is not a foolproof remedy for poor work. Although peer review can be a valuable tool for improving a work product, it cannot be relied upon to ensure excellence in a product that is seriously lacking in technical merit when it enters peer review.

Peer reviewers are human and therefore can occasionally be narrow, parochial, biased, over-committed, or mistaken.

Peer review cannot ensure that regulatory policies and actions will be based on "good science." It can only seek to assess and to aid in improving the technical merit and validity of the scientific and analytical information that is made available to government decision-makers. Peer review does not control what they do with that information. It is inevitable that much of the decision-making in any government agency is part of a process influenced by legislation, the courts, value judgments, ideology, politics, and efforts to accommodate stakeholders. Good scientific input to a decision cannot ensure that the decision will be based on good science if the science is ignored or outweighed by other considerations.

Peer review of original scientific articles submitted to journals has received some study in recent years, but there has been no rigorous study of the processes, benefits, and limitations of peer review of regulatory documents or the science that underlies them. Public debate about peer review in this context is often characterized by strong opinion, self-interest, and selected anecdotal evidence.

Peer-Review Policy Developments at EPA

Under the Federal Advisory Committee Act, the Environmental Research, Development, and Demonstration Act, and other statutes, several standing groups of highly qualified experts from outside EPA periodically review various scientific and technical practices, policies, and activities of the agency. These groups include EPA's Science Advisory Board (SAB) and its independently chartered subgroups, the Clean Air Scientific Advisory Committee (CASAC), the Advisory Council on Clean Air Act Compliance Analysis (ACCAACA), and the Federal Insecticide, Fungicide, and Rodenticide Act (FIFRA) Scientific Advisory Panel, as well as the Office of Research and Development (ORD) Board of Scientific Counselors (BOSC). These groups conduct their reviews and meetings in public and document their findings and recommendations extensively.

ORD, by virtue of its scientific staff and mission, has been familiar and comfortable with peer-review processes and has used them effectively for assessing and improving research publications and for various other purposes since the agency was created in 1970. Peer review has been a central feature of ORD's competitive research-grant program since that program was initiated in 1980, and ORD has had a formal peer-review policy in place since 1982 (40 CFR Part 40).

Some of the other offices of EPA have relied on scientific and technical information to various degrees, have substantial numbers of scientists on staff, and have utilized peer review in limited ways for many years. Prime examples are the Office of Prevention, Pesticides, and Toxic Substances; the Office of Air Quality Planning and Standards; and parts of the Office of Water. However, in some other parts of EPA, scientific activities and the use of peer review have not traditionally been prominent, and over the years, EPA has been criticized many times for having a poor scientific basis for many of its regulatory decisions (Powell 1999).

In 1991, EPA Administrator William Reilly requested a panel of four academic scientists, including two members subsequently appointed to our committee, to evaluate how EPA could meet the goal of using sound science as the foundation for agency decision-making. Their report, *Safeguarding the Future: Credible Science, Credible Decisions* (EPA 1992), reported that a perception existed that EPA lacked adequate safeguards to prevent the unacceptable practice of adjusting science to fit policy. The panel recommended that an independent program of quality assurance and peer review be instituted and applied to the planning and results of *all* scientific and technical efforts to obtain data used for guidance and decision-making at EPA. This program would be applied not only to the research products of ORD, most of which were already being peer reviewed, but also to many activities and work products in the agency's regulatory program and regional offices, including model development and use, data collection and evaluation, monitoring plans, research, technical studies, scoping studies, and assessments. The panel considered such a program to be essential if EPA was to be perceived as a credible, unbiased source of environmental information.

In 1993, in response to those recommendations, Administrator William Reilly issued a policy memorandum that embraced the peer-review recommendations of the *Safeguarding the Future* report and promulgated an agency policy statement developed by EPA's then-existing Council of Science Advisors (Reilly 1993). The policy strengthened and expanded the peer-review process in agency activities, but at the same time it specified that managers in the agency's programs should retain flexibility and discretion to apply peer review in the context of "program priorities and operating constraints."

In his 1993 memorandum, Administrator Reilly noted that the process of peer review and other forms of peer involvement enable the agency to harness the knowledge of far more experts than those within the agency to improve the quality of its programs, documents, and decisions. He also noted that agency managers should maintain sufficient discretion to accommodate their program priorities and operating constraints, and he acknowledged a tension between peer review and the control of agency actions. He directed that major scientific and technical work products related to agency decisions should normally be peer reviewed, but that agency managers would continue to be accountable for decisions about when and how to utilize peer review. He noted specifically that peer review cannot be a substitute for required federal notice-and-comment requirements on rule-makings and adjudicative procedures. He requested the appointment of an agency working group to address implementation issues. Work products considered "non-major" and non-technical were specifically excluded from the policy, but those items were not defined.

In February 1994, the General Accounting Office (GAO) issued a report entitled *Peer Review: EPA Needs Implementation Procedures and Additional Controls* (GAO 1994) that found agency-wide peer-review practices to be deficient in several ways. It pointed out that the 1993 policy statement had not defined the technical products to be reviewed, and that implementation of the policy was being impeded by concerns among various EPA offices about the diversity of technical products and the scope, timing, cost, confidentiality, available expertise, and other aspects of reviews. The GAO reported a lack of consistent understanding, uniform procedures, and accountability mechanisms for peer review around the agency.

In June 1994, Administrator Carol Browner issued a peer-review policy statement that "reaffirmed the central role of peer review" in EPA (Browner 1994). The statement acknowledged concerns about the agency's lack of a comprehensive peer-review program, updated former-Administrator Reilly's 1993 statement on peer review, and articulated broad principles that remain in effect today. The 1994 statement designated EPA's Science Policy Council to coordinate the expansion and improvement of peer-review practices throughout the agency. It directed all EPA offices and regions to develop standard operating procedures for peer review and to work with the Science Policy Council in identifying "major scientific and technical work products" that should be required to undergo peer review. It described peer review as ranging broadly from informal consultations with previously uninvolved EPA staff colleagues (internal peer review) to external peer reviews by such groups as the EPA SAB or FIFRA Science Advisory Panel. While stating that major scientific and technical work products related to agency decisions "normally should be peer-reviewed," the policy statement delegated to individual managers in the agency's headquarters offices, regions, laboratories, and field components the responsibility and accountability for deciding in individual circumstances whether to use peer review, and if so, deciding its "character, scope, and timing." It cautioned that formal peer review should not be conducted in a manner that caused EPA to miss statutory or court deadlines.

In July 1994, an EPA agency-wide steering committee recommended strengthening the use of peer review throughout the agency (EPA 1994b), and in October 1994, EPA's ORD reported to Congress that it planned to work with the National Science Foundation to improve its peer review process for extramural grants and would expand the use of peer review in other areas, including research plans, research contracts, cooperative agreements, interagency agreements, laboratory programs, intramural laboratory proposal competitions, research investigator performance, and research work products (EPA 1994c).

In March 1995, our committee expressed support for those actions of EPA and for ORD's stated plans to strengthen and expand its uses of peer review for both work products and plans (NRC 1995b). We recommended that an appropriate set of peer-review procedures be developed and applied with strong presumptions favoring peer review, the involvement of external experts, and the nomination of such experts by independent referees instead of project managers. We recommended that peer review be applied to intramural and extramural research projects and programs, including research conducted by EPA scientists and engineers at ORD laboratories and centers, as well as extramural research conducted by others (or cooperatively with others) through individual investigator grants, multidisciplinary grants, research centers, other cooperative agreements, interagency agreements, fellowships and training grants, on-site research support contracts, and other research contracts.

In September 1996, the GAO reported that EPA's implementation of its 2-year-old peer-review policy remained "uneven" (GAO 1996). The GAO acknowledged some improvements in peer-review practices, especially in ORD, but it attributed the spotty performance across other offices of the agency to misunderstanding of the nature, requirements, and benefits of peer review by many agency staff and managers, and also to inadequate mechanisms of oversight and accountability for peer review in EPA. The GAO selected and considered nine EPA scientific and technical documents that it judged to require peer review; and it concluded that EPA's peer-review policy had been fully followed for only two of them, not fully followed for five, and not conducted at all for two, including EPA's critically important Mobile Source Emissions Model, which was subsequently reviewed by the National Research Council (NRC 2000) at the request of Congress. The GAO observed that EPA's peer-review oversight mechanisms essentially consisted of a two-part reporting scheme in which each office and region annually self-nominated products for peer review and updated the status of previously nominated products. The GAO argued that agency managers were being given too much leeway to avoid conducting peer reviews without adequate, documented justification. It recommended that managers be required to catalog all major scientific and technical work products, the plans for review of each, and the reasons why any of them were not chosen to be reviewed.

In response to the GAO report, EPA's deputy administrator asked the assistant administrator for research and development, in consultation with the other assistant administrators, to develop procedures for reviewing peer-review decisions and ensuring adequate peer reviews on all major scientific and technical documents throughout the agency (Hansen 1996). An agency-wide evaluation of peer-review implementation was initiated early in 1997. The evaluation was mainly conducted by ORD through case studies and interviews with cognizant managers and staff across the agency. It discovered a considerable variety of approaches, understandings, and attitudes around EPA with respect to peer review. Although it found some excellent examples of peer-review practices, it confirmed the GAO's finding of misunderstanding in various quarters and found that some offices were not considering all agency activities or the agency's regulatory agenda in identifying major products to be considered for review.

The problem was perhaps exemplified in the case of EPA's mathematical models. Many EPA rule-makings rely substantially on mathematical models that attempt to predict toxic risk, exposure, emissions, or other variables. It is important that the design, assumptions, and validation of such models be carefully peer reviewed. In response to concerns raised by the SAB in 1989 and a 1994 report of an agency task force on mathematical modeling for regulatory uses, ORD organized a "Models 2000" workshop, held in December 1997 in Athens, GA. At that workshop, many EPA staff members involved in developing and applying such models indicated that agency peer-review policies had not been followed and were not even widely understood.

In February 1998, Administrator Browner and Deputy Administrator Hansen issued a new peer-review handbook (EPA 1998a) to replace the standard operating procedures that had been developed by individual offices and regions in response to the administrator's June 1994 peer-review policy statement (Browner 1994). The new handbook, developed in an agency-wide effort under the leadership of EPA's Science Policy Council, was designed to provide uniform implementation guidance to managers and staff in the agency's offices, regions, and laboratories for peer review of the 2,000 major scientific and technical work products per year estimated to require such review across the agency.

The handbook acknowledges that peer reviews at EPA take many different forms depending on the nature of the work product, statutory requirements, and office-specific policies and practices. In question-and-answer format with flowcharts and checklists, the new handbook provides guidance on basic principles and definitions, including distinctions between peer review and peer input, public comment, and stakeholder involvement; planning and preparing for peer review, including the identification of "major scientific and technical" work products, appropriate peer-review mechanisms, and qualified experts; and conducting peer reviews, including materials required, record-keeping, and the utilization of peer review comments.

It specified three categories of annual reporting from each EPA office and region: (a) a cumulative list of products reviewed since 1991 with a short summary of the review; (b) a list of candidate products for future review; and (c) a cumulative list of products for which a decision has been made not to review, with a brief description of the reasons for not reviewing it. The lists are to indicate the names of all decision-makers and dates of decisions concerning peer review.

The 1998 handbook reiterated that the agency's assistant administrators and regional administrators were responsible for peer reviews within their programs. It authorized these officials to delegate various responsibilities to subordinate managers and designated staff peer-review coordinators in each office and region. It assigned a special role to the assistant administrator for research and development to monitor and assist the other offices in ensuring adherence to the guidelines. The deputy administrator was identified as having ultimate responsibility for peer review across the agency and for arbitrating any conflicts or concerns about peer review.

In June 1999, Acting Deputy Administrator Peter Robertson instituted a new requirement that all action memoranda from EPA assistant administrators accompanying rule-makings submitted to the administrator for approval must include a statement certifying compliance with the agency's peer-review policies (Robertson 1999).

In November 1999, the Research Strategies Advisory Committee of the SAB reported that the agency has shown "diligence" with respect to peer review, that its peer-review process is "well-articulated," "fundamentally sound," and "with a few exceptions, working as intended" (EPASAB 1999). It concluded that EPA has been responsive to previous recommendations of the SAB, the GAO, and other organizations regarding peer review. It commented that EPA's peer-review processes are continuing to improve through high-level management commitment and a mechanism of continued internal examination and process changes led by the agency's ORD and Science Policy Council.

WHAT DOCUMENTS ARE PEER REVIEWED?

EPA's overall policy on peer review states (Reilly 1993; Browner 1994),

Major scientific and technically based work products related to Agency decisions normally should be peer reviewed. Agency managers within Headquarters, Regions, laboratories, and field components determine and are accountable for the decision whether to employ peer review in particular instances and, if so, its character, scope, and timing. These decisions are made in conformance with program goals and priorities, resource constraints, and statutory or court-ordered deadlines. For those work products that are intended to support the most important decisions or that have special importance in their own right, external peer review is the procedure of choice. Peer review is not restricted to the penultimate version of work products; in fact, peer review at the planning stage can often be extremely beneficial.

As discussed in the previous section, this policy led to the development of the *Peer Review Handbook* by EPA's Science Policy Council (EPA 1998a). Both the 1994 policy and the 1998 handbook concentrate on the peer review of "major scientific and technical work products" that affect agency decisions, although the 1994 policy also encouraged the review of certain planning documents.

The peer-review handbook provides detailed guidance on deciding what documents should be peer reviewed (Figure 3-1). It specifies that peer review should be conducted on scientific and technical work products that support a research agenda, regulatory program, policy position, or other agency position or action. Such work products may

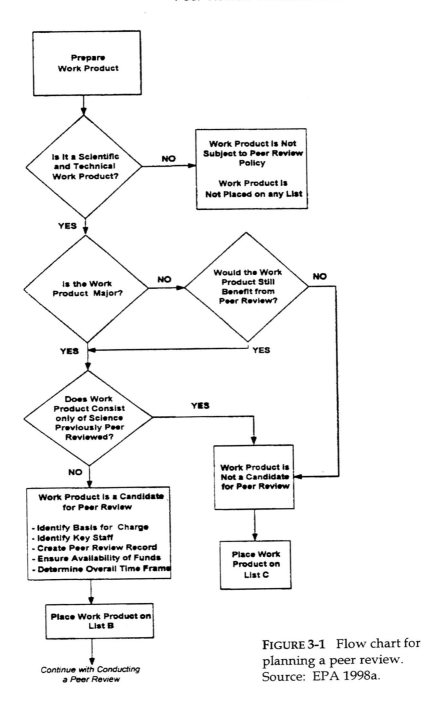

FIGURE 3-1 Flow chart for planning a peer review. Source: EPA 1998a.

include risk assessments, technical studies and guidance, analytical methods, scientific database designs, technical models, technical protocols, statistical studies, technical background materials, technical guidance, and research plans and strategies. Examples of work products not to be reviewed are documents addressing procedural matters or policy statements. For work products supporting rule-making actions or site-specific regulatory decisions, the handbook specifies that the peer review should be performed on the scientific or technical document, not the rules, regulations, or decisions themselves. It specifies that scientific and technical work products supporting major rules, including rules determined to be "significant" by the Office of Management and Budget under Executive Order 12866, should be closely scrutinized.

In determining whether a scientific or technical work product warrants peer review, section 2.2.3 of the handbook allows case-by-case decisions to be made by agency officials but identifies several criteria for such judgments. These criteria include work products that significantly establish or depart from a precedent, model, or methodology; address novel, controversial, or emerging issues; have cross-agency or interagency implications; involve substantial resources; take innovative approaches; or satisfy statutory or other legal mandates for peer review. The handbook concludes overall that when there is doubt about whether to peer review a work product, the decision should be to make it a candidate for review.

Section 2.2.4 of the handbook includes certain categories of economics in its definition of work products needing review. They include guidance documents for conducting economic analysis; new economic methodologies; novel applications of economic methods; and broad-scale economic assessments of regulatory programs. The handbook envisions that peer reviews of such work products will normally be conducted independently by the Environmental Economics Advisory Committee, a subgroup of EPA's SAB.

Section 2.3 of the handbook exempts certain categories of work products from peer-review requirements, including derivative summaries or compendiums of previously peer-reviewed products or preliminary analyses subsequently replaced by peer-reviewed products. In addition, the handbook allows that in rare cases, statutory or court-ordered deadlines or financial constraints may limit or preclude peer review of major scientific or technical work products that would otherwise be required to undergo review. Decision-makers are required to document justification for such decisions.

ORD has had a formal peer-review policy in place since 1982. As befitting a scientific organization, ORD utilizes peer review in many ways. Its current peer-review practices address not only the end-products of scientific work, but also research strategies and plans, research proposals, ongoing laboratory programs, research staff performance, fellowship applications, and other items.

Although the Research Strategies Advisory Committee (RSAC) of the SAB recently judged the agency's peer-review handbook to be "an excellent guidance document" that "provides definitive criteria for deciding what to peer review," it expressed concern that the current mechanisms for deciding whether to peer review a particular product might in some cases be unduly influenced by available funding, timing constraints, and pressures to complete the product (EPASAB 1999).

On the basis of a review of EPA's lists of documents reviewed, chosen as candidates for future review, or considered but not chosen for review, the RSAC generally concluded that "the right products are being peer reviewed," although it expressed uncertainty about whether some of the products classified as "not for peer review" should have been reviewed (EPASAB 1999). The RSAC cautioned that decisions to review or not to review a product are not always being documented consistently, and it stressed the importance of transparency in EPA's process of deciding the subjects and mechanisms of peer review.

The RSAC also recommended that the agency expand its peer-review practices beyond the "major scientific and technical work products" specified in the 1994 peer-review policy statement and defined in the peer-review handbook (EPASAB 1999). In particular, the RSAC recommended that EPA also apply peer review

- to interagency and international work products considered important to environmental decision-making;
- not only to final work products but also to early review of significant scientific and technical planning products, such as strategic plans, analytical blueprints, research plans, and environmental-goals documents;
- to social-science research and work products instead of only natural-science work products; and
- to policy analysis documents that are not purely science-based

but involve the application of policy and values to ensure that appropriate methods and procedures have been used, including an explicit treatment of assumptions and value judgments, adequate sensitivity analysis, and adequate treatment of uncertainty.

The RSAC judged the omission of planning documents to be an important deficiency in the agency's peer-review handbook. It pointed out that peer review early in a project can have a significant impact on the direction of the effort and the quality of the final product. It observed that changes can often be made more easily in the planning stages of an activity than in the final-product stage, when there might be more resistance to change and greater deadline pressures.

Our committee generally concurs with the RSAC recommendations. Some of those recommendations already are being addressed to some extent in EPA's peer-review program. For example, Section 2.2.10 of the handbook specifies review of scientific and technical work products produced by organizations other than EPA when they are used in EPA decision-making. Also, the administrator's 1994 peer-review policy statement states, "Peer review is not restricted to the penultimate version of work products; in fact, peer review at the planning stage can often be extremely beneficial." Section 2.2.1 of the 1998 handbook includes research plans and strategies among the work products requiring review, and ORD now does that routinely. Nevertheless, the other EPA offices have often failed to submit planning documents to peer review, and this NRC committee believes that greater emphasis in the agency's peer-review handbook on the categories of documents identified by the SAB could help improve the scientific and technical basis for agency actions.

FORMS AND MECHANISMS OF PEER REVIEW

Although Administrator Browner's 1994 peer-review policy statement directed that major scientific and technical work products related to agency decisions "normally should be peer-reviewed," it delegated to individual managers in EPA headquarters offices, regions, laboratories, and field components the responsibility and accountability for deciding in individual cases whether to use peer review, and if so, deciding its "character, scope, and timing." It cautioned that formal peer review should not be conducted in a manner that caused EPA to miss statutory or court deadlines.

EPA's 1998 peer-review handbook provides detailed guidance on choosing the form and planning the conduct of peer reviews (Figure 3-2). It devotes considerable discussion to some issues that apparently had not been well understood in some parts of the agency. For example, it emphasizes that peer review is not "peer input," sometimes called "peer consultation"—the involvement of experts, even outside experts, in the development of a work product—because adequate impartiality and detachment cannot be assumed for experts who participated in the creation of a document, even parts of it. It states that no amount of peer input can substitute for peer review by independent, third-party experts. It further stressed that peer review is not stakeholder input or consensus building; it is important to get the science correct before the values and policies are negotiated. It also distinguished peer review from public comment, such as that required by the Administrative Procedures Act or other statutes and obtained through the *Federal Register* or other means. It emphasized that peer review requires evaluation by individuals carefully chosen for relevant expertise and should focus on technical issues, whereas public comment is open to all individuals and all issues.

The handbook emphasizes that the greatest credibility is provided when peer reviewers are external to the agency and the peer-review process is formal. However, it acknowledges that peer reviews at EPA might take many forms and allows substantial flexibility in determining the forms and mechanisms of peer reviews, depending on the importance and complexity of a work product; the relevant statutory and judicial deadlines and other requirements; the financial resources; and the office-specific policies and practices.

Section 2.4.2 of the handbook provides examples of the kinds of external and internal peer review that may be conducted. External-review mechanisms may include reviews by individual outside experts; ad hoc groups of outside experts; agency-sponsored peer-review workshops; groups established under the Federal Advisory Committee Act, such as the SAB, FIFRA Science Advisory Panel, Clean Air Scientific Advisory Committee, or ORD Board of Scientific Counselors; special boards or commissions; interagency committees; committees convened by other agencies; or nongovernmental groups such as the National

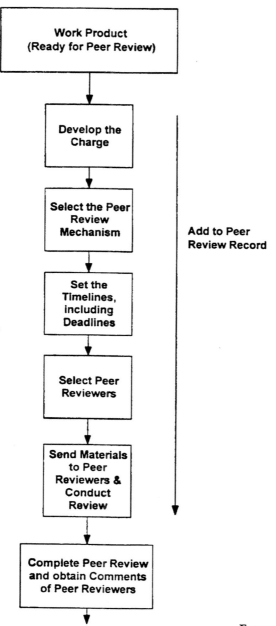

FIGURE 3-2 Flow chart for conducting a peer review. Source: EPA 1998a.

Academy of Sciences or the Society of Risk Analysis. Internal-review mechanisms allowed by the handbook include reviews by experts from ORD or other offices of the agency or ad hoc panels of experts from the agency.

For scientific and technical work products supporting major rules, including rules determined to be "significant" by the Office of Management and Budget under Executive Order 12866, the handbook emphasizes that external peer review is the procedure of first choice, and any decision to use internal peer review for such work products, although acceptable in some circumstances, should be the exception rather than the rule.

While generally praising EPA's 1998 peer-review handbook and program, the RSAC of the SAB recently cautioned that the agency needs to ensure that the process does not become "inappropriately bureaucratic" (EPASAB 1999). It stressed the importance of keeping the focus of the peer-review process on the improvement and credibility of scientific products. It emphasized the need to avoid making peer-review requirements seem punitive or wasteful. ORD's BOSC reached a similar conclusion in its 1998 program review of the National Center for Environmental Research and Quality Assurance (EPABOSC 1998e). The BOSC expressed concern that peer-review and quality-assurance procedures in some cases might become or be seen by others as bureaucratic burdens that did not produce added value commensurate with their cost.

Our committee concurs with the above findings of the SAB and the BOSC. As discussed at the beginning of this chapter, peer review must be viewed and used as a tool for improving quality. It must become accepted as a part of the agency's culture, not merely a bureaucratic requirement. Steps should be taken to foster this cultural change (e.g., regular dissemination of the benefits of completed reviews).

The committee recommends that the Science Policy Council's reviews of the agency's peer-review handbook and experience with its implementation include an explicit focus on promoting appropriate forms and levels of review for different types of work products and on reducing unnecessarily complex or inefficient requirements. The Science Policy Council should not necessarily wait the 5-year interval specified in the peer-review handbook; it should make changes as needed. The agency cannot afford to allow unnecessary or inefficient requirements to continue so long. The Science Policy Council's review should be ongoing. We also recommend that the Science Policy Council review a true random sample of peer-reviewed work products, examining the decisions made in structuring the review, the responses to review, and the cost, quality, timeliness, and impact of the review.

SELECTION OF PEER REVIEWERS

The 1998 peer-review handbook specifies that it is fundamental to the peer review process that reviewers be technically qualified — professional peers of the authors whose work is reviewed. The handbook also emphasizes that peer reviewers should be independent — not associated with the development of the work product, either through substantial contribution to its development or through significant consultation during its development.

Section 1.4.8 of the 1998 handbook specifies that peer reviewers are expected to perform their role with objectivity, as free as possible from institutional or ideological biases or financial conflicts of interest, although it notes that in many cases, some of these requirements might be impossible to meet or might not promote the best possible reviews. In such cases, the deliberate selection of some reviewers with offsetting biases can be appropriate and even necessary. Such cases should be fully disclosed. In many peer-review systems, reviewers are asked to maintain confidentiality to promote candor and to protect the authors whose work is being reviewed, but some peer reviews, such as those performed by EPA's SAB or other groups under the Federal Advisory Committee Act, are conducted openly.

Section 1.4.9 of the handbook allows EPA staff to be considered "independent" reviewers if such staff are in a different organizational unit of EPA and outside the chain of command of the responsible decision-maker.

In September 1999, EPA's Office of Inspector General issued a report stating that, in some cases, the management controls in place were insufficient to ensure that EPA program offices and contractors adequately screened peer reviewers for independence and potential conflict of interest (EPA 1999b). From a sample of 32 work products scheduled for review in 1997 or 1998, the report identified several cases in which EPA program offices or contractors had not attempted to determine potential conflict of interests or had not properly documented their determinations. However, the report acknowledged that these instances might have occurred before the implementation of, or staff training on, the 1998 peer-review handbook. The Inspector General recommended that ORD supplement the handbook with additional guidance and training materials on the independence of peer reviewers, including any financial relationships with EPA, and ORD agreed to do so. The Inspector General also recommended that agency contracts should include specific provisions requiring contractors to address concerns about the independence of peer reviewers. The Inspector General also commented that some of the peer-review schedule information reported by program and regional offices to ORD was inaccurate. ORD responded that a new peer-review database, which became operational in July 1999, is expected to reduce such errors, and the SAB Research Strategies Advisory Committee recently commented that Section 3.4 of the 1998 peer-review handbook contains "good guidance on issues related to conflict of interest for the peer reviewers" (EPASAB 1999).

Our committee considers the most important resource required for a good peer-review program to be the availability of qualified expert reviewers who are willing and able to perform the reviews. The limits to this resource can be important. In its site visit to the ORD Extramural Center, members of our committee were informed that the review of STAR research grant applications alone requires the efforts of more than 1,000 peer reviewers per year, and EPA's Science Policy Council has estimated that over 2,000 major scientific and technical work products affecting agency actions currently require such review each year. That means EPA must identify and obtain the services of many thousands of expert reviewers annually. It is important to maximize the benefits from their efforts.

DOCUMENTATION AND RESPONSE TO PEER REVIEWS

EPA's 1998 peer-review handbook specifies that the completion of a peer review requires careful evaluation of reviewers' comments and recommendations, utilization of reviewers' comments to complete the final work product, and creation of a record of the review. The handbook provides guidance on each of these requirements (Figure 3-3).

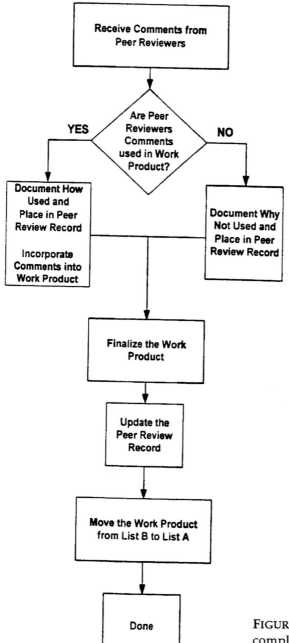

FIGURE 3-3 Flow chart for completing a peer review. Source: EPA 1998a.

The designated peer-review leader is responsible for assessing the validity and objectivity of all comments in consultation with other agency staff and, as appropriate, agency management. For each peer review conducted, the handbook requires the creation of a peer-review record that includes information such as the draft work product submitted for review; the charge and other materials given to the reviewers; the comments and other information received from the reviewers; materials prepared in response to the reviewers' comments, indicating acceptance or rebuttal and nonacceptance of the comments; the final work product revised in response to review; and other (e.g., logistical) information about the review.

The effectiveness of peer review in the improvement of a scientific or technical work product obviously depends not only upon the independent expert evaluations, but also upon what is done in response to those evaluations. If the criticisms and suggestions received from independent peer reviewers are to some degree ignored or taken lightly by decision-makers who might be more concerned about meeting a deadline or producing a desired answer than enhancing technical merit, then the benefits of peer review are compromised. On the other hand, in most types of peer reviews, there is no requirement for a consensus among the reviewers. In fact, there is no requirement to accommodate all reviewers' comments. Reviewers can be mistaken. But the integrity and value of the peer-review process depends critically on thoughtful and conscientious consideration and application of the comments.

MANAGEMENT AND OVERSIGHT OF PEER REVIEWS

In 1996, the GAO observed that EPA's peer-review oversight mechanisms essentially consisted of a two-part reporting scheme in which each office and region annually self-nominated products for peer review and updated the status of previously nominated products (GAO 1996). The GAO argued that agency managers were being given too much leeway to avoid conducting peer reviews without having to justify the decisions. It recommended that managers be required to catalog all major scientific and technical work products, the plans for review of each, and the reasons why any of them were not to be reviewed.

In response, EPA's deputy administrator initiated an ongoing "audit" that was assigned to the Quality Assurance Division of ORD's National Center for Environmental Research and Quality Assurance to evaluate on an ongoing basis the extent to which the agency's offices and regions were complying with the administrator's 1994 peer-review policy. The agency's 1998 peer-review handbook reinforced this ongoing evaluation by requiring that decisions on whether to peer-review any scientific or technical work product be documented through the agency's annual peer-review reporting process. As specified in Section 1.3.2 of the handbook, three lists are maintained: (a) a cumulative list of work products peer reviewed since 1991, (b) a list of candidate products for future peer review, and (c) a list of products for which a decision has been made not to undergo peer review. The lists contain information on each work product, such as the responsible EPA office or region, peer-review leader, agency decision-maker, review mechanism, review dates or schedule, a summary of the review, and comments on the review process or a rationale for not conducting a peer review. The handbook specifies that the designated peer-review coordinator for each EPA office or region is responsible for organizing an annual review of all peer review activities in that office or region and providing it to ORD according to annual guidance issued by the EPA deputy administrator.

Pursuant to the EPA administrator's 1994 peer-review policy statement, the agency's Science Policy Council is responsible for overseeing agency-wide implementation of the policy. This oversight includes an ongoing responsibility to interpret the policy, assess its implementation, and revise the policy as necessary. The Science Policy Council has established a peer-review advisory group to assist it in carrying out these responsibilities.

Section 1.4 of the 1998 handbook specifies that the assistant administrator or regional administrator in charge of an EPA office or region is ultimately accountable for implementing the peer-review policy in his or her respective organizations, and that the EPA deputy administrator is ultimately responsible for peer review across the agency, including final arbitration of any conflicts or concerns about peer review. Section 1.4 also defines the roles of "decision-makers," "peer-review coordinators," and "peer-review leaders." Although the assistant administrator or regional administrator is the ultimate decision-maker for each peer review, the handbook allows this role to be delegated to subordinate office directors, division directors, or even project managers. The decision-maker is responsible for determining whether a work product gets reviewed, determining what peer-review mechanism to use, ensuring the necessary time and resources for the review, and ensuring the proper performance and documentation of the review or decision not to review a work product. The peer-review coordinator is the staff member responsible for monitoring and overseeing all peer-review activities within a given EPA office or region, coordinating peer-review training, mediating difficult issues, ensuring proper record-keeping on peer reviews, and functioning as the office or regional peer-review liaison with ORD and the Science Policy Council. For each peer review (i.e., the review of each work product), the decision-maker designates a peer-review leader. Section 1.4.4 of the handbook allows the decision-maker or the project manager for a work product to be the peer-review leader. The peer-review leader is responsible for organizing, overseeing, and documenting the individual review, including selecting and instructing the peer reviewers and responding to the reviews. Either directly or through an agent such as the SAB or a contractor, the peer-review leader is to select peer reviewers with appropriate expertise and independence, as specified in Section 1.4.8 of the peer-review handbook, and write an appropriate charge to the reviewers, including information on the purpose of the material to be reviewed, its potential use in agency decision-making, and the key scientific and technical findings and issues. The peer-review leader or agent should be trained in peer-review practices and should understand the scientific content and issues in the material to be reviewed.

The 1998 peer-review handbook also emphasized the importance of proper planning for peer review, stating that peer review "needs to be incorporated into the up-front planning of any action based on the work product—this includes obtaining the proper resource commitments (people and money) and establishing realistic schedules." It recognized that peer review unavoidably adds to the time and cost of a project and should be realistically planned into the project. The handbook provided a "manager's planning checklist" for this purpose (Figure 3-4).

In 1999, the SAB began a multiyear effort to assess the peer-review program in EPA. In the first report resulting from this effort, the SAB

Managers Planning Checklist for Peer Review

1)   **Title of Work Product:** _____

2)   **What Decision/Rule/Regulation/Action Does this Work Product Support:** _____

_____

3)   **Determination of Major Scientific and Technical Work Products**
☐ Is the work product scientific or technical __yes __no?
☐ Is the work product __major or __non-major?

4)   **Determining What Peer Review is Needed**
☐ If major, peer review is needed
☐ If not major, is peer review still needed
☐ When does the review need to be done?
☐ How much time will be needed to conduct/complete the review?
☐ Are there court ordered deadlines or other constraints?
☐ Has senior management (AA/RA/others) been informed of progress/problems?
☐ What would constitute success for this review?

5)   **Determining the Resources for Peer Review**
☐ What is the priority of this project relative to other projects in the same office?
☐ What resources are needed to conduct the review?
☐ What are the impacts of the review on personnel?
☐ Who will lead the peer review?
☐ Who will conduct the peer review?
☐ Who will maintain the peer review record?
☐ Where will the peer review record be kept?
☐ What mechanism will be used for the peer review?
☐ Has the charge been developed?
☐ Has internal and external coordination been initiated/completed?
☐ Have arrangements for interim/final sign-offs (e.g., for the charge, the panel, on any changes to the final work product) been made?
☐ How will results of the review be presented and addressed in the final work product (e.g., in a preamble, in an accompanying appendix -- as well as changes in the work product itself)?
☐ Has the work product been entered onto List B or C, as appropriate?

6)   **Comments:** _____

FIGURE 3-4 Managers planning checklist for peer review. Source: EPA 1998a.

praised "the Agency's diligence" and high-level management commitment to peer review" (EPASAB 1999). It judged EPA's peer-review process to be "well established" and that it "is well articulated and appears to be fundamentally sound and, with a few exceptions, working as intended." It noted that EPA's peer-review program is "continuing to improve through a mechanism of continued internal examination, led by the Office of Research and Development and . . . the Science Policy Council." The SAB emphasized that a key to success in implementing the peer-review process has been the involvement of ORD in the oversight role, and that "ORD scientists have an understanding of the importance of peer review in developing good scientific and technical products." The SAB noted favorably ORD's effective role in the development and implementation of peer-review training, collection of data on products and their review status, and bench-marking of EPA's peer review efforts against reviews at other organizations. The SAB plans to continue conducting an in-depth assessment of trends in EPA's uses of peer review, the impacts of the peer reviews, and additional opportunities for enhancing the benefits from peer review in the form of quality, credibility, relevance, and the agency's leadership position.

The SAB expressed concern about potential conflict of interest on the part of designated peer-review leaders, noting that current agency policy, as stated in Section 1.4.4 of the peer-review handbook, allows an agency decision-maker on a particular work product to be the peer-review leader (EPASAB 1999). Such a manager might have a special interest in the outcome of the review and might therefore be unable to ensure the essential degree of independence of a peer review. The SAB compared this policy to the agency's data-quality-assurance practices, in which a quality-assurance staff officer is empowered to stop activity if there is a quality-assurance problem. It recommended that peer-review leaders be similarly empowered to stop a work product from moving forward if a peer review has not been properly completed. In addition, it recommended that agency staff be required to complete appropriate training before being designated as a peer-review leader.

EPA has made excellent progress in expanding and strengthening its peer-review practices, and in most respects, EPA's 1998 peer-review handbook is consistent with the recommendations of a previous NRC report (NRC 1998b). However, our committee concludes that the agency should find a way to ensure a greater degree of independence in the management of its peer reviews. The committee acknowledges that it is appropriate for the agency's peer-review policies and handbook to afford flexibility to accommodate statutory and court deadlines and resource limitations, and this committee does not disagree with EPA's policy of holding the assistant administrators, regional administrators, and subordinate managers in the agency's regulatory programs accountable for peer review. Nevertheless, independence is essential to the proper functioning of the peer-review process, and EPA's current policies fail to ensure adequate independence. Our committee shares the SAB's concern about the potential conflicts of interest of EPA peer-review leaders and decision-makers.

Therefore, our committee recommends that EPA change its peer-review practices to more strictly separate the management of a work product from the management of the peer review of that work product. The committee believes that the decision-maker and peer-review leader for a work product should never be the same person, and that wherever practicable, the peer-review leader should not report to the same organizational unit as the decision-maker. Although the decision-maker should retain the authority to overrule provisionally any decisions or objections from a peer-review leader, with the final decision to be made by the EPA administrator, the independent decisions and any objections of a peer-review leader should be preserved and made a part of the agency decision package and public record for a work product. If such an independent assessment produces criticism of the adequacy or outcome of a peer review, EPA's policy should be to ensure that such criticism is clearly noted, divulged, and explained.

For completed research work products, our committee encourages ORD to continue and to expand its longstanding practice of urging the in-house and extramural research scientists it supports to publish their research in peer-reviewed journals that meet international standards of scientific quality. To the extent possible, intramural and extramural research supported by EPA should be published in peer-reviewed journals that are open to scientific and public scrutiny. When such publication is not possible (e.g., when the volume of the research results that are important to the agency is so large that the pertinent results cannot be accommodated in a peer-reviewed journal), panels of experts should make an evaluation of quality that is essentially equivalent to that of the peer-reviewed scientific literature. Evaluations should include scientists and engineers from outside ORD and also outside EPA.

4

Strengthening Science at EPA

THIS chapter summarizes and integrates our committee's most important findings and recommendations concerning research management and peer-review practices and presents related recommendations concerning scientific leadership at EPA. These findings and recommendations are based on the committee's consideration of the matters discussed and documents cited in the preceding chapters of this report and the work and reports of the Committee on Research Opportunities and Priorities for EPA—our companion committee in this study. Members of our committee made many site visits to EPA's laboratories, centers, and headquarters and regional program offices, as listed in the first chapter of this report. In addition, several members of our committee have gained considerable knowledge of EPA research-management and peer-review practices through participation in previous and ongoing reviews of various scientific activities in EPA under the auspices of the NRC, the SAB, the BOSC, and other organizations.

Based on all these factors, *the committee concludes that the following broad themes and the recommendations associated with them, as presented below, are of paramount importance to the goal of strengthening the scientific performance of ORD and the agency overall:*

- *scientific leadership and talent;*
- *research continuity and balance;*

- *research partnerships and outreach;*
- *research accountability; and*
- *scientific peer review.*

SCIENTIFIC LEADERSHIP AND TALENT

In the 30 years since EPA was created, the agency's scientific practices and performance have been criticized many times in reports from the NRC, EPA's SAB, the General Accounting Office, and many other organizations; in congressional oversight and judicial proceedings; and in countless criticisms and lawsuits from stakeholders with interests in particular EPA regulatory decisions. In one such report, *Safeguarding the Future: Credible Science, Credible Decisions* (EPA 1992), a panel of academicians, including two members of our committee, concluded, "Currently, EPA science is of uneven quality, and the Agency's policies and regulations are frequently perceived as lacking a strong scientific foundation." While acknowledging that EPA had a number of knowledgeable scientists on its staff, the panel reported that the science base at EPA was not *perceived* to be strong by the university community, and that many EPA scientists at all levels throughout the agency believed that EPA did not use their scientific knowledge and resources effectively. The panel further observed "A perception exists that regulations based on unsound science have led to unneeded economic and social burdens, and that unsound science has sometimes led to decisions that expose people and ecosystems to avoidable risks." The panel commented that EPA had not always ensured that contrasting, reputable scientific views were well-explored and well-documented from the beginning to the end of the regulatory process. It pointed out that the agency was often perceived to have a conflict of interest because it needed science to support its regulatory activities, and it described a widely held perception by people both outside and inside the agency, that EPA science was "adjusted" by EPA scientists or decision-makers, consciously or unconsciously, to fit policy.

As discussed in many places throughout this report, EPA has made significant improvements in some of its scientific practices since that panel issued its report in 1992. However, the committee concludes that there is a continuing basis for many of the scientific concerns raised in that panel's report and others, such as the 1999 Resources for the Future report *Science at EPA: Information in the Regulatory Process* (Powell 1999). We base this conclusion on the extensive experience of the members of our committee in assessing EPA's scientific practices and performance, including the matters discussed and documents cited in this report and other independent investigations of EPA science in which members of our committee have participated.

The creation of a new position of science advisor to the administrator of EPA was one of the principal recommendations of the 1992 report. It envisioned that the essential function of the science advisor would be to ensure that EPA policy decisions are informed by a clear understanding of relevant science. The panel recommended that the new science advisor advise the EPA administrator, implement a peer-review and quality-assurance program for all EPA science-based products; be a key player when EPA makes a policy decision, ensuring that the science and uncertainties relevant to a policy or regulatory issue are considered; play a key role in evaluating the professional activities of EPA scientists; reach out to the broader scientific community for information; and maintain an appropriate relationship with EPA's SAB. The panel suggested that the role of the new science advisor might be somewhat analogous to the role of the general counsel, who will not approve a document destined for an external audience until it is judged legally defensible.

The 1992 panel considered two models: the science advisor could be either a senior scientist on the EPA administrator's staff, chosen by each administrator, or the assistant administrator in charge of EPA's research office (or a deputy to that official). In assessing those options, the panel observed that a science advisor on the administrator's staff would be more likely to have a relationship of confidence with the administrator but might be somewhat removed from scientists throughout the agency and unable to direct resources to address scientific issues. In comparison, the assistant administrator for EPA's research program would command considerable resources but in some cases might be involved in a conflict of responsibilities as the administrator's science advisor (e.g., when ORD's work products or program budget were being evaluated). And a deputy to the assistant administrator for ORD might suffer the additional handicap of not being sufficiently senior to exercise a strong role in the inner counsels of the administrator.

In response to the 1992 report, Administrator Reilly appointed a science advisor on his immediate staff. Although the individual selected was highly qualified and was able to secure some accomplishments in his brief tenure, that individual was never given the authority that would be required to perform the agency-wide role envisioned by the 1992 panel concerning the improvement of EPA's scientific credibility. The science-advisor position did not survive long after the 1993 change in administration and is currently vacant.

Throughout EPA's history, no official below the level of the administrator has had overall responsibility or authority for the scientific and technical foundations of agency decisions, and administrators of EPA have typically been trained in law, not science. The agency's most senior science official has traditionally been the assistant administrator for research and development, but that official has never had agency-wide responsibility or authority for overseeing the scientific and technical basis for regulatory and policy decision-making, and EPA's regulatory offices are not required to follow scientific advice from ORD. That is a formula for weak scientific performance in the agency and poor scientific credibility outside the agency.

In our interim report (NRC 1995b), this committee recommended "that the assistant administrator for research and development be designated as EPA's chief scientific and technical officer, responsible not only for ORD, but also for coordinating and overseeing agency-wide scientific policy, peer review, and quality assurance, as well as EPA's outreach to the broader domestic and international scientific community for scientific knowledge relevant to the agency's mission." Shortly thereafter, in partial response to that recommendation, the deputy administrator of EPA asked the head of ORD to coordinate the agency's scientific-planning and peer-review activities.

Although the 1995 designation appears to have been a small step in the right direction, our committee judges it to be insufficient. First, the head of ORD was not given real authority for agency-wide scientific policy. Second, although the agency subsequently achieved some commendable progress through its interoffice Science Policy Council and ORD-led efforts to begin developing an agency-wide inventory of scientific activities and a "Strategic Framework for EPA Science," all those efforts, relying on consensus and voluntary cooperation of the agency's regulatory and regional offices in the absence of central science-policy authority, have had slow and limited success. The heads of EPA's regulatory and regional offices are of equal rank to the head of ORD and are generally not required to follow ORD's guidance regarding scientific activities or science policy. Third, the ability of the head of ORD to coordinate agency-wide peer-review and quality-assurance practices was diminished in 1999 with the reassignment of some peer-review functions from ORD to the agency's newly created Office of Environmental Information.

Furthermore, based on our observations of these developments in the five years since our interim report, the committee has become convinced that our 1995 recommendation to designate the head of ORD as EPA's chief scientific and technical officer also was insufficient. The committee now concludes that it underestimated in 1995 the level of authority needed to achieve the necessary degree of cooperation and coordination of scientific activities and policy in the regulatory and regional offices. In addition, the committee has become more aware of the enormous amount of scientific activity occurring in EPA's regulatory and regional offices, and it concludes that no single individual could reasonably be expected to direct a world-class research program in ORD while also trying to improve scientific practices and performance throughout the rest of the agency. These jobs are inherently different. Moreover, assigning agency-wide scientific authority to the assistant administrator for ORD might produce a conflict of responsibilities, because many decisions about science in the regulatory programs could affect ORD's budget or favor ORD's research over research done elsewhere.

Based on many of the issues discussed in this report and the extensive experience of the members of our committee with scientific practices in EPA, the committee concludes that EPA needs an appropriately qualified scientific official at a sufficiently high level to carry both the authority and responsibility for agency-wide scientific performance. No official below the level of deputy administrator could perform this role. The requisite operating authority with accountability for agency-wide scientific performance cannot be met by assigning the scientific gate-keeper function to any assistant administrator, including that of ORD, regardless of the qualifications or abilities of the individual holding that position. It is unrealistic to expect that an official at that level could effectively coordinate and oversee the scientific and technical programs and work products of other EPA offices and regions, especially while also carrying out the important duties of directing a first-rate research program. EPA needs a top science official with the authority and responsibility to obtain and use the best possible science in support of the agency's mission and to identify the scientific uncertainties and conflicting evidence relevant to the agency's regulatory and policy decisions.

The importance of science in EPA decision-making should be no less than that afforded to legal considerations. Just as the advice of the agency's general counsel is relied upon by the administrator to determine whether a proposed action is "legal," an appropriately qualified and adequately empowered scientific official is needed to attest to the administrator and the nation that the proposed action is "scientific" — that it is consistent, or at least not inconsistent, with available scientific knowledge — and that the agency has done a proper job of ascertaining and applying that knowledge and recognizing and characterizing the relevant uncertainties. Achieving these goals will require a level of accountability for EPA's scientific performance that cannot reasonably be expected from an administrator who is not trained in science, a staff advisor to the administrator without line authority, or an assistant administrator for research and development who has no authority over the use of scientific information by other offices of the agency.

Therefore, to enhance the effective and appropriate use of science in EPA and the agency's scientific credibility, *the committee recommends the establishment of a new position at EPA: deputy administrator for science and technology.*

This position would require authorization from Congress, appointment by the President, and confirmation by the Senate. The current position of deputy administrator might become deputy administrator for policy and management. The new deputy administrator for science and technology would have the following principal responsibilities:

- Ensure that the most important scientific issues facing EPA are identified and defined, including those embedded in major policy or regulatory proposals.
- Develop and oversee an agency-wide strategy to acquire and disseminate the necessary scientific information either through

intramural efforts or through extramural programs involving academia, other government agencies, and the private sector in this country and abroad.

- Ensure that the complex scientific outreach and communication needs of the agency are met, including the need to reach throughout the agency for credible science in support of the regulatory offices, regions, and agency-wide policy deliberations, as well as the need to reach out to the broader domestic and international scientific community for scientific knowledge that is relevant to an agency policy or regulatory issue.
- Coordinate and oversee scientific quality-assurance and peer-review activities throughout the agency, including activities in support of the regulatory and regional offices.
- Develop processes to ensure that appropriate scientific information is utilized in decision making at all levels in the agency.
- Ensure and, in effect, certify to the administrator and the nation that the scientific and technical information used in each EPA regulatory decision and policy is valid, appropriately characterized in terms of scientific uncertainty and cross-media issues, and appropriately applied.

The deputy administrator for science and technology would perform all of the roles envisioned by the *Safeguarding the Future* panel (EPA 1992). This official would coordinate and oversee the agency's Office of Research and Development, the newly-created Office of Environmental Information, Science Advisory Board, Science Policy Council, and scientific and technical activities in the agency's regulatory program and regional offices.

The individual appointed to this position would need to have an outstanding background, including research experience, experience in public forums, and the respect of scientific peers, administrative peers, and legislators.

The creation of this position would send a strong message that Congress and the administration are committed to strengthening science at EPA.

The position of next importance to EPA's scientific performance and reputation is the assistant administrator for ORD. Over the years, there has been occasional debate on whether the assistant administrator for

ORD should continue to have a political appointment or a longer-term statutory appointment. It is sometimes argued that a political appointment ensures that the head of ORD will have power in budget negotiations similar to that of the politically appointed heads of EPA's regulatory and regional offices. However, although the political aspect of the assistant administrator's job often receives considerable attention, the most important aspects of the job are not political. Besides running ORD, the assistant administrator is responsible for representing EPA's research program to the world's scientific community, interpreting the agency's research and development program to the public, and maintaining a national and international watch on major environmental science and engineering developments.

Under the present political-appointment model, the leadership of ORD changes at least as often as the administration changes. Historically, the typical tenure of ORD assistant administrators has been only about 2 or 3 years. Frequent changes in the leadership of ORD have been disruptive and have led to devastating effects on the continuity of programs and the morale of ORD scientists and staff. Over the years, the assistant administrator for ORD has typically been one of the last senior EPA officers appointed in a new administration, and although ORD has had some very capable assistant administrators, there have been a few cases in which little weight seems to have been given to the candidate's scientific or managerial qualifications.

Therefore, to foster greater continuity in the management of EPA's research program, *the committee recommends that the position of assistant administrator for ORD be converted to a statutory term appointment of 6 years.*

The assistant administrator for ORD should have an advanced degree in an appropriate scientific or technological discipline, a substantial record of scholarly achievement, and administrative experience that includes successful management of a substantial research program. The position should be defined to make it attractive to an eminent scientist or engineer who is willing to remain in the position for a sufficiently long period of time to bring stability to the direction and leadership of ORD. A statutory term appointment would make the position more like those of the leaders of NIH or NSF. Congressional action would be required to convert the position to a 6-year term.

Any organization that aspires to excellence must have effective leadership at many levels, not just at the top. Criteria for the selection and advancement of managers at all levels in ORD laboratories and centers should favor research managers who not only are capable managers and supervisors, but also are scientifically and technically accomplished. They should understand the work and have the respect of their research staff while having the ability to select, inspire, lead, and otherwise encourage other scientists and engineers in their endeavors. They should also be strong advocates and defenders of the continuity and core capabilities required for the conduct of a good research program. EPA's ability to recruit, develop, and retain such leaders depends on many factors, including the agency's commitment and success in reducing bureaucratic impediments and finding ways to increase the flexibility afforded to research managers to fulfill their responsibilities.

The committee recommends that ORD make a concerted effort to give its research managers a high degree of flexibility and accountability. They should be empowered to make decisions at the lowest appropriate management level consistent with EPA policy and ORD's strategic goals and budget priorities.

ORD and EPA should make a special effort to resist a tendency commonly seen in large institutions to impose cumbersome bureaucratic procedures in response to management concerns. Bureaucratic paranoia, fault-finding, and fear of possible fault-finding can paralyze and demoralize an organization. Excessively bureaucratic procedures are antithetical to a creative research program with a high standard of quality, efficiency, and teamwork. ORD should frequently examine itself to identify and eliminate excessive bureaucratic safeguards, administrative hurdles, redundant requirements for approvals at multiple levels of management, and other bureaucratic impediments.

Research leaders at all levels in ORD should strive to minimize bureaucratic impediments, provide timely responses to requests from other organizations and from staff scientists and engineers, and place high priority on finding ways to increase flexibility in getting research done. ORD managers throughout the organization should be given the authority and resources to make decisions at the lowest appropriate level of management, provided that such decisions are compatible with EPA policies and ORD's strategic goals and budget priorities. Decisions that might fit within this category include research problem selection; acquisition of most equipment and supplies, personnel assignment; staff attendance at scientific meetings; inviting and supporting visiting scientists; and granting permission and support for ORD scientists to work for a time in another laboratory in this country or abroad.

To achieve scientific and technical excellence, ORD, EPA, or any other institution must also attract, retain, and properly support first-rate, dedicated professionals on its staff. Our committee is aware of many outstanding scientists and engineers in ORD and other parts of the agency. As discussed in Chapter 2, the committee's site visits were especially encouraging in that regard, and the committee concurs with the judgments expressed by ORD's BOSC (EPA BOSC 1998a-e) concerning the substantial number of highly capable and productive staff members in ORD's laboratories and centers.

The ORD work force is aging. More than 47% of ORD's employees are 50 years old or older, and more than 550 ORD employees will be eligible to retire within the next 5 years. Periodic EPA hiring freezes, combined with intense scientific and technical job-market competition from the private sector and academic institutions, are making it extremely difficult for ORD to recruit the new talent needed to sustain and enhance its research work force.

The committee commends ORD for the excellent fellowships program it has developed. This program has brought a stream of fresh scientific and technical talent into EPA's research program and is helping to train future research leaders in environmental science, engineering, and other disciplines.

The committee recommends that ORD continue to place high priority on its graduate fellowship and postdoctoral programs.

The 1992 *Safeguarding the Future* report recommended that ORD recruit and support on a long-term basis four to six senior research scientists and engineers with world-class reputations in areas vital to EPA's long-term strategy and direction. The panel envisioned that these eminent scientists and engineers would serve as examples and mentors for all scientists in EPA and would bring access to networks of world-class scientists to benefit the agency. The panel recommended that EPA's SAB be asked to form a search committee.

As discussed in Chapter 2, ORD responded to this recommendation by obtaining and using special authority to recruit and promote research scientists and engineers to senior, nonmanagerial positions — so-called "ST" (scientific and technical) positions at the Senior Executive Service level — using merit-review panels that include outside experts to evaluate candidates. ORD now has eight such individuals in its laboratories.

Our committee fully supports ORD's use of the "ST" program and urges that it be continued. However, recognizing today's intense job-market competition with industry and academic institutions for top research talent, the committee concludes that even greater measures are warranted and practicable to attract and retain outstanding research scientists and engineers in the ORD laboratories.

In research, perhaps even more than in other fields, pre-eminent leadership sets the standard and tone for the rest of the work force. A single world-class investigator can generate ideas and enthusiasm to elevate a research program dramatically. In research, leadership is not synonymous with management or administration.

The committee recommends that ORD create the equivalent of endowed academic research chairs in the national laboratories.

This might be accomplished by awarding prestigious 5-year renewable grants or distinguished fellowships to distinguished academic scientists to work at ORD laboratories; the committee suggests that it is not necessary for all such researches to be regular federal employees. Alternatively, ORD could seek authority to create and fill positions similar to NIH Title 42 senior research appointments, perhaps in connection with internal grants to ensure sustained research support for these distinguished investigators. The SAB or the BOSC should be asked to assist ORD in developing this program and selecting the candidates.

Using such mechanisms, ORD should recruit at least one additional distinguished investigator per laboratory in areas of research that are rapidly advancing and important to ORD's future. These individuals should be given maximum intellectual freedom to pursue potentially productive lines of research that are consistent with laboratory missions and ORD priorities. The distinguished investigators should be expected to serve as mentors and role models for other ORD research scientists but should have no managerial responsibility beyond their own research teams.

The committee supports ORD's use of individual development plans for each professional staff member. The plans, negotiated between an employee and supervisor, address career paths, training, and rotational goals. The committee also supports the work of ORD's Human Resources Council to help managers at all levels address staff support and morale issues, including efforts to reduce bureaucracy, improve two-way communication between management and staff, provide career-development opportunities, and address infrastructure problems.

RESEARCH CONTINUITY AND BALANCE

Frequent changes in goals, priorities, practices, structure, or funding can disrupt any organization, but they are especially damaging to a research organization, which has special requirements for continuity in the development and maintenance of scientific and engineering talent, experience, and infrastructure if it is to be productive. Maintaining the requisite degree of stability in ORD has been a continuing challenge due to many expansions and other changes in EPA's legislative mandates and priorities, directives from Congress and different administrations, pressures from regulated parties and other interest groups, lawsuits and court decisions, inadequate budgets to meet competing demands, and changes in the leadership of ORD and EPA.

ORD has changed its research goals, priorities, and practices often and abruptly in the past. Greater stability, continuity, and predictability are among the most important needs in the ORD program. Becoming competent in a particular line of research requires a large investment of time, effort, and often dollars that often cannot be readily shifted to some new area of concern. The limited financial and human resources of ORD should be managed with a steady hand and a clear and persistent vision of how to invest its resources to maximize the long-term gains in scientific understanding resulting from its work.

Our committee's interim report (NRC 1995b) endorsed the general scope and direction of ORD's 1995 reorganization, in which ORD adopted as a principal organizing concept the reduction of uncertainty in risk assessment and risk management, initiated a new strategic research planning process, consolidated its laboratories and centers, and expanded and strengthened its research grants, centers, fellowships, and peer-review programs. Our interim report called these the most important changes in the history of EPA's research program. In the long run, the courses ORD set for itself in 1995 should have a stabilizing effect on the research program, and our committee continues to support them. In many respects those changes are still a work in progress, and they need more time to mature.

Therefore, in addition to converting the position of assistant administrator for ORD to a statutory term appointment of 6 years, as recommended in the previous section of this chapter, *the committee recommends that ORD continue steadily on the courses it set in the 1995 reorganization.*

In the past few years, ORD has explored a multiyear approach for research planning to foster continuity and strategic integration of some research efforts. ORD has developed multiyear plans for its particulate-matter research program, as recommended by another NRC committee (NRC 1998a), and also for research on endocrine disruptors, drinking water, environmental monitoring, global climate change, and pollution prevention. Multiyear plans for additional areas of research are under development. The plans are developed by research teams from ORD laboratories and centers and are peer reviewed. Our committee expects that ORD's recent efforts in multiyear planning will contribute greatly to research program continuity and the achievement of strategic goals, and ORD merits commendation for these initiatives.

The committee recommends that ORD continue and expand its multiyear research planning approaches in both problem-driven and core research areas.

As recommended by our companion committee (NRC 1997), ORD also needs to maintain a balance between problem-driven research and technical support for the agency's regulatory programs, and the core research to better understand and anticipate environmental risks. These roles are not unrelated or incompatible; they are mutually reinforcing. Core research is the indispensable wellspring that prepares and enables ORD to provide better problem-specific research and technical assistance to the agency and the nation.

ORD should meet the continuing challenge to lead the agency by means of research while continuing to assist its client regulators who have variable levels of understanding or appreciation of science but a strong say in ORD's budget and priorities. Activities in support of regulatory programs often have a narrow focus and often compete to preempt long-term research programs. They tend to consume the resources of a research organization disruptively and disproportionately. Regulatory strategies, which are typically prescriptive and specific, tend to freeze concepts and methods in time, and the more closely that ORD is tied to the regulatory programs, the greater the risk that ORD will to some extent be working on outdated problems or with outdated approaches.

On the other hand, using ORD for problem-driven research and technical assistance to regulatory and regional offices has important benefits. Perhaps the greatest dividends are the resulting improvements in the scientific aspects of the agency's regulatory decisions and the maintenance of an in-house scientific core group experienced in dealing with environmental risks and programs. An experienced scientific core group can be of great value in meeting emergency requirements for technical expertise. ORD's technical assistance provides the regulatory offices with competent scientific help, and it enables ORD's research scientists to keep abreast of regulatory and policy developments elsewhere in EPA.

The committee concurs with the recommendations of the 1997 report of its companion committee—the Committee on Research Opportunities and Priorities for EPA—that ORD should maintain approximately an even balance between core research and problem-driven research.

RESEARCH PARTNERSHIPS AND OUTREACH

From time to time the question arises whether EPA should have its own research program or rely on research results developed elsewhere. Advocates of having the research conducted elsewhere often cite past criticisms of the agency's research program and point to excellent research programs of other agencies, such as NIH, NSF, and the Department of Energy, that collectively, and in some cases individually, dwarf that of EPA. And, of course, the academic community and the private sector conduct much of the research relevant to EPA's mission.

In the 1992 report *Safeguarding the Future: Credible Science, Credible Decisions,* a panel of four senior academicians, including two members of our committee, concluded that EPA needs its own strong science base to provide the background required for effective environmental protection programs. Similarly, *Building a Foundation for Sound Environmental Decisions*, the 1997 report of the NRC's Committee on Research Opportunities and Priorities for EPA — our companion committee in this study — concluded that EPA needs a strong in-house research program.

Our committee agrees that a vigorous research program should be maintained in EPA. Moving the research program out of the agency would most likely weaken, not strengthen, the scientific foundation of EPA's decisions and actions. Although some abstract concept of scientific "quality" might be improved by reducing some kinds of ORD technical work that are unlikely to advance research frontiers, such work is often critically necessary to EPA's pursuit of its mission and statutory responsibilities. Overall, eliminating ORD or moving its functions out of EPA would be destructive, and the level of damage would increase with passing time as EPA became increasingly unable to pursue, apply, or even understand new research knowledge. An EPA devoid of a research program would not be likely to attract substantial scientific talent, and an EPA without scientific talent would be ineffective and potentially harmful to the nation.

However, even with a much larger budget, ORD could not meet all the vast and constantly expanding needs of EPA and the nation for scientific and technical knowledge to guide environmental protection efforts. ORD has had a first-rate research program in some important areas, such as aquatic toxicology and human inhalation toxicology, but it is not possible for ORD to be a leader across the full range of scientific knowledge required by EPA. EPA should recognize the limits of its research capabilities. It should be a leader in some areas of research, involved in other selected areas, and well-informed in all areas relevant to the agency's mission. As discussed in Chapter 2, ORD has been criticized at times for failing to obtain and apply the results of research performed elsewhere.

The committee recommends that ORD place greater emphasis on maintaining awareness of research conducted by other organizations. ORD should develop and implement a pro-active, structured, and visible strategy for stimulating, acquiring, and applying the results of research conducted or sponsored by other federal and state agencies, universities, and industry, both in this country and abroad.

The strategy should include increased sabbatical assignments for

ORD researchers to gain experience in other scientific organizations, and more visiting appointments of scientists and engineers from universities, other government agencies, and private organizations to work in ORD laboratories and centers.

ORD's expanded and strengthened competitive research grants and centers programs have greatly increased the number and activities of talented academic researchers across the nation engaged in research relevant to EPA's mission. The committee commends ORD for its excellent performance in developing and implementing these programs, as well as for the partnerships it has built with other agencies and funding organizations in joint grant solicitations. However, as discussed in Chapter 2, questions have been raised about the adequacy of the numbers and skill mix of the staff of ORD's National Center for Environmental Research who administer the research grants, centers, and fellowships programs. Since 1995, ORD has increased the research-grant funds administered by the center by about 400% without substantially increasing the center's staff. This has placed high demands on the staff who are responsible for the review process and the monitoring and dissemination of grantees' research products. The committee recognizes that the staff who manage EPA's STAR grants program must perform additional roles beyond those of NSF grants officers, because of the mission-relevance and technology-transfer requirements of the STAR program.

The committee recommends that the numbers and skill mix of the staff of ORD's National Center for Environmental Research be reassessed to ensure they are consistent with the needs of the current program of research grants, centers, and fellowships.

The committee encourages strengthening the interactions between STAR grantees and research scientists and engineers in the ORD laboratories. At present, there are insufficient mechanisms for facilitating such interactions. One possible mechanism might be to ask grant applicants to identify in their proposals how their research might be enhanced by interactions with EPA scientists and how their research might complement or supplement ongoing or planned research in the ORD laboratories. Reviewers of the proposals, as well as ORD scientists and the SAB, could also be asked for suggestions.

The committee recommends that the National Center for Environmental Research, in concert with ORD's national laboratories, de-

velop additional mechanisms to promote and facilitate research inter-actions among STAR grantees and ORD research staff.

Safeguarding the Future: Credible Science, Credible Decisions (EPA 1992) concluded that the academic community, Congress, other federal agencies, industry, the public, and even many within EPA are generally unfamiliar with the work of EPA scientists. The 1992 panel emphasized that many officials involved in funding EPA science were uncertain about what science products EPA had produced, and whether the quality and quantity of its products were commensurate with the dollars expended. It noted that EPA's policy and regulatory work receives a great deal of public attention, but the agency's science typically receives a similar degree of attention only when the scientific basis for a decision is questioned. The panel concluded that EPA should strive to make more widely known the short-term and long-term scientific goals and achievements of its research laboratories, contractors, and grantees. It urged the agency to develop and implement a coherent communications, outreach, and education plan to publicize the activities and accomplishments of EPA scientists.

Even within the agency, many regulatory and regional program officials throughout EPA's history have been largely unaware and even dubious of any important benefits from ORD's research program, and consequently they have not been supportive of ORD's budget. Recently, the GAO reported that one of EPA's regulatory program offices so acutely needed information on ORD's work (relevant to its program), well beyond the progress reports that ORD was providing, that the regulatory office found it necessary to pay for the development of a system to track ORD's projects (GAO 1999). That kind of situation is not healthful for ORD or the agency. ORD's ongoing efforts to disseminate its research products and inform others about them have, with some exceptions, been meager and unimaginative.

The committee recommends that EPA substantially increase its efforts to disseminate actively ORD's research products and ongoing projects, to explain their significance, and to assist others inside and outside the agency in applying them.

Publication of original research articles is critically important, but it is not sufficient. EPA should publish more individual research-topic-area summaries and comprehensive annual summaries of the results of its in-house and extramural research and technical support activities.

The summaries should be planned and tailored for specific audiences and should emphasize potential applications by other EPA offices, state agencies, industry, and others.

In addition, our committee concurs with the 1998 recommendation of ORD's BOSC that the National Center for Environmental Assessment should revise its mission to focus more on being an advisor, catalyst, and resource for the risk assessments performed by the rest of the agency, rather than trying itself to do individual risk assessments with its own limited resources. The center should focus on being a research organization dedicated to advancing the state of practice in risk assessment. It should reduce its role as a performer of individual risk assessments that could be done by EPA's regulatory offices.

RESEARCH ACCOUNTABILITY

In commenting on ORD's fiscal year 2000 budget, the SAB indicated that the lack of transparency in the decision-making process used by ORD to set research priorities made it difficult to evaluate the adequacy of the proposed budget. The ORD strategic plan describes general processes and criteria by which decisions are made on research priorities and funding allocations, but only in very broad terms.

During the committee's site visits and interviews, the staff of some EPA regulatory program offices expressed the belief that they have little influence on ORD's research priorities through the Research Coordination Council or any other mechanism. They felt that they needed a stronger voice in the setting of ORD's priorities, and that ORD should be held more accountable to the agency's other offices for performing agreed-upon tasks.

In addition to the work performed in its in-house laboratories, ORD has a number of available mechanisms for extramural funding, including interagency agreements, contracts, grants, cooperative agreements, and fellowships. Each of these mechanisms has its own advantages and limitations. ORD's strategic plan (EPA 1996a, 1997a) lists several factors that are typically considered in making decisions about who will perform each research activity in ORD laboratories or outside the agency. These factors include the nature of the work, who has the appropriate expertise, how urgently the results are needed, the degree to which the work must be specified or can be made flexible, the available in-house capacity, the potential value of involving multiple institutions, and the opportunities for funding leverage. The process by which ORD decides whether a project or task is to be performed by in-house staff or through one or more of these extramural mechanisms is of crucial importance to the quality of the work and the cost-effective management of resources. Unfortunately, this decision-making process has not been sufficiently open or visible for persons outside ORD or EPA to reconstruct or assess how the decisions were made.

The committee recommends that ORD substantially improve the documentation and transparency of its decision-making processes for setting research and technical-assistance priorities, making intramural and extramural assignments, and allocating funds.

ORD should continue to be responsive to the agency's regulatory offices for the problem-driven and technical-assistance components of its program, and the agency's regulatory offices should continue to have a strong voice in decisions about the ORD plans and budget elements devoted to those components. For the core-research portion of its program, however, ORD should have greater freedom to set the agenda, without the need for specific concurrence of regulatory program offices that are focused on statutory requirements and regulatory goals. In the agency planning process, ORD should continue to consider the views and needs of the program offices in developing both components of its program, but it should maintain an adequate degree of independence in planning a core-research program that will successfully perform the leadership and anticipatory-research role that such a program can bring to the agency.

ORD's research should not be the only scientific studies held accountable in EPA. A great deal of research-like activity, including many activities in scientific and technical data-gathering, analysis, and interpretation, are being conducted or funded by EPA offices outside ORD. Much of this work is not labeled "research." The other offices of EPA do not have the kind of authorization that ORD has to conduct research per se, and full disclosure might risk the loss of control of such activities by the regulatory offices. Historically, many of the scientific studies and analysis performed or funded outside ORD have not been fully coordinated across the agency or included in ORD's research-planning and peer-review programs. Our committee is by no means opposed to scientific studies and analyses being conducted in parts of the agency outside ORD, but such activities require transparency, quality assurance, and accountability, just as ORD's program does.

ORD, with the help of others throughout the agency, has begun to develop an inventory of science projects and programs across EPA. Our committee commends EPA for this important step. We recommend that the preliminary inventory be expanded to include information well beyond its current scope, such as goals and objectives of the projects, milestones, schedules, principal investigators and project managers, and allocations of staff and financial resources.

The committee recommends that the administrator direct the deputy administrator for science and technology to expand upon the agency's recently initiated science inventory by conducting, documenting, and publishing a more comprehensive and detailed inventory of all scientific activities conducted by agency units outside ORD. The results of the inventory should be used to ensure that such activities are properly coordinated through the agency-wide science-planning and budgeting process and are appropriately peer reviewed.

The inventory should include information well beyond its current scope — information such as project goals, milestones, schedules, principal investigators and project managers, and allocations of staff and financial resources. The SAB should be engaged in overseeing this inventory effort.

SCIENTIFIC PEER REVIEW

The committee congratulates EPA and its Science Policy Council for the excellent progress it has made in strengthening and expanding the agency's peer-review practices. The agency's 1998 peer-review handbook, discussed in Chapter 3, is a valuable resource and guidance document. In most respects, the handbook is consistent with the recommendations of a previous NRC report on peer-review practices (NRC 1998b).

EPA's SAB has expressed concern about potential conflicts of interest on the part of peer-review leaders — individuals assigned to manage reviews of agency work products — because current agency policy allows the same individual to be a project manager for the development of a particular work product and the peer-review leader for the same work product (EPA SAB 1999). Obviously, such a manager might have, or be perceived to have, a special interest in the outcome of the review and might therefore be unable to ensure the essential degree of independence. The SAB contrasted this policy with the agency's data-quality-assurance practices, in which a staff officer is empowered to stop activity if there is a quality-assurance problem. It recommended that peer-review leaders be similarly empowered to stop a work product from moving forward if a peer review has not been properly completed.

EPA has made excellent progress in expanding and strengthening its peer-review practices, but the agency should find a way to ensure a greater degree of independence in the management of its peer reviews. The committee acknowledges that the agency should have adequate flexibility to accommodate statutory and court deadlines and resource limitations. Nevertheless, independence is essential to the proper and credible functioning of the peer-review process, and EPA's current policies fail to ensure adequate independence. Our committee shares the SAB's concern about the potential conflicts of interest of EPA peer-review leaders and decision-makers. Despite good intentions, and even if the current policy works well much of the time, it is inevitable that some of these individuals, under great pressure to meet a deadline or implement a regulatory policy, are tempted to compromise the integrity of the peer-review process for some work products by making convenient or improper decisions on the form of peer review, the selection of reviewers, the specification of charges to the reviewers, or the responses to reviewers' comments.

The committee recommends that EPA change its peer-review policy to more strictly separate the management of the development of a work product from the management of the peer review of that work product, thereby ensuring greater independence of peer reviews from the control of program managers, or the potential appearance of control by program managers, throughout the agency.

The committee believes that the decision-maker and peer-review leader for a work product should never be the same person, and that wherever practicable, the peer-review leader should not report to the same organizational unit as the decision-maker. Although statutory and judicial deadlines might make it necessary that a program-office decision-maker retain the authority to proceed with an action on a provisional basis despite objections or concerns from a peer-review leader, with the final decision to be made by the EPA administrator, the independent decisions and any objections of a peer-review leader should be preserved and made a part of the agency decision package and public record for a work product. If such an independent assessment produces criticism of the adequacy or outcome of a peer review, EPA's policy should be to ensure that the criticism is clearly noted, divulged, and explained.

The committee also recommends that the Science Policy Council's reviews of the agency's peer-review handbook and of experiences with its implementation include an explicit focus on promoting appropriate forms and levels of review for different types of work products and on reducing unnecessarily complex or inefficient requirements. The Science Policy Council should not necessarily wait the 5-year interval specified in the peer-review handbook; it should make changes as needed. The agency cannot afford to allow unnecessary or inefficient requirements to continue so long. The Science Policy Council's review should be ongoing. We also recommend that the Science Policy Council review a true random sample of peer-reviewed work products, examining the decisions made in structuring the review, the responses to review, and the cost, quality, timeliness, and impact of the review.

Finally, the committee wishes to emphasize that peer review must become accepted throughout EPA as a part of the agency's culture—a tool for improving quality—not merely a bureaucratic requirement. Measures such as periodic dissemination of the impacts and benefits of completed reviews might help to foster this cultural change in the agency.

References

Browner, C.M. 1994. Memorandum to Assistant, Associate and Regional Administrators; General Counsel; Inspector General; and Staff Office Directors. Peer Review Program. Peer Review and Peer Involvement at the U.S. Environmental Protection Agency. Office of the Administrator, U.S. Environmental Protection Agency, Washington, DC. June 7.

Budde, W.L. 1997. "Good turmoil" at EPA Labs. Environ. Sci. Technol. 31(4):166A-167A.

Carnegie Commission on Science, Technology, and Government. 1992. Environmental Research and Development: Strengthening the Federal Infrastructure. New York: Carnegie Commission. 143 pp.

CEQ (U.S. Council on Environmental Quality). 1970. Environmental Quality: the First Annual Report of the Council on Environmental Quality. Washington, DC: U.S. Government Printing Office. 326 pp.

EPA (U.S. Environmental Protection Agency). 1992. Safeguarding the Future: Credible Science, Credible Decisions. The Report of the Expert Panel on the Role of Science at EPA. EPA/600/9-91/050. U.S. Environmental Protection Agency, Washington, DC.

EPA (U.S. Environmental Protection Agency). 1993. Report to Congress: Fundamental and Applied Research at the Environmental Protection Agency. EPA/600/R-93/038. Office of Research and Development, U.S. Environmental Protection Agency, Washington, DC.

EPA (U.S. Environmental Protection Agency). 1994a. Report to Congress FY 1994: Fundamental and Applied Research at the Environmental Protection Agency. EPA/600/R-94/040. Office of Research and Development, U.S. Environmental Protection Agency, Washington, DC.

EPA (U.S. Environmental Protection Agency). 1994b. Research, Development, and Technical Services at EPA: A New Beginning. Report to the Administrator. EPA/600/R-94/122. U.S. Environmental Protection Agency, Washington, DC.

EPA (U.S. Environmental Protection Agency). 1994c. Report to Congress: Development of Peer Review Systems at EPA. Interim Report. Office of Research and Development, U.S. Environmental Protection Agency, Washington, DC.

EPA (U.S. Environmental Protection Agency). 1996a. Strategic Plan for the Office of Research and Development. EPA/600/R-96/059. Office of Research and Development , U.S. Environmental Protection Agency, Washington, DC.

EPA (U.S. Environmental Protection Agency). 1996b. Particulate Matter Research Program Strategy. External Review Draft. NHEERL-MS-97-019. Office of Research and Development, U.S. Environmental Protection Agency, Research Triangle Park, N.C. Available: http://www.epa.gov/ordntrnt/ORD/resplans/oldresplans.html

EPA (U.S. Environmental Protection Agency). 1997a. 1997 Update to ORD's Strategic Plan. EPA/600/R-97/015. Office of Research and Development, U.S. Environmental Protection Agency, Washington, DC.

EPA (U.S. Environmental Protection Agency). 1997b. EPA Strategic Plan. EPA/190-R-97-002. Office of the Chief Financial Officer, U.S. Environmental Protection Agency, Washington, DC.

EPA (U.S. Environmental Protection Agency). 1997c. Research Plan for Microbial Pathogens and Disinfection By-Products in Drinking Water. EPA 600-R-97-122. Office of Research and Development, U.S. Environmental Protection Agency, Cincinnati, OH.

EPA (U.S. Environmental Protection Agency). 1998a. EPA Science Policy Council Handbook: Peer Review. EPA 100-B-98-001. Office of Science Policy, Office on Research and Development, U.S. Environmental Protection Agency, Washington, DC.

EPA (U.S. Environmental Protection Agency). 1998b. Research Plan for Arsenic in Drinking Water. EPA/600/R-98/042. Office of Research and Development, U.S. Environmental Protection Agency, Cincinnati, OH.

EPA (U.S. Environmental Protection Agency). 1998c. Research Plan for Endocrine Disruptors. EPA/600/R-98/087. Office of Research and Development, U.S. Environmental Protection Agency, Research Triangle Park, N.C.

EPA (U.S. Environmental Protection Agency). 1998d. Ecological Research Strategy. EPA/600/R-98/086. Office of Research and Development, U.S. Environmental Protection Agency, Washington, DC.

EPA (U.S. Environmental Protection Agency). 1998e. Pollution Prevention

Research Strategy. EPA/600/R-98/123. Office of Research and Development, U.S. Environmental Protection Agency, Cincinnati, OH.

EPA (U.S. Environmental Protection Agency). 1999a. Waste Research Strategy. EPA/600/R-98/154. Office of Research and Development, U.S. Environmental Protection Agency, Cincinnati, OH.

EPA (U.S. Environmental Protection Agency). 1999b. Office of Inspector General Survey Report: EPA's Selection of Peer Reviewers. 1999-P-217. U.S. Environmental Protection Agency, Washington, DC.

EPABOSC (U.S. Environmental Protection Agency Office of Research and Development, Board of Scientific Counselors). 1998a. Program Review of the National Exposure Research Laboratory (NERL). Final Report. April 30.

EPABOSC (U.S. Environmental Protection Agency Office of Research and Development, Board of Scientific Counselors). 1998b. Program Review of the National Health and Environmental Effects Research Laboratory (NHEERL). Final Report. U.S. Environmental Protection Agency, Washington, DC. April 30.

EPABOSC (U.S. Environmental Protection Agency Office of Research and Development, Board of Scientific Counselors). 1998c. Program Review of the National Risk Management Research Laboratory (NRMRL). Final Report. U.S. Environmental Protection Agency, Washington, DC. April 30.

EPABOSC (U.S. Environmental Protection Agency Office of Research and Development, Board of Scientific Counselors). 1998d. Program Review of the National Center for Environmental Assessment (NCEA). Final Report. U.S. Environmental Protection Agency, Washington, DC. April 30.

EPABOSC (U.S. Environmental Protection Agency Office of Research and Development, Board of Scientific Counselors). 1998e. Program Review of the National Center for Environmental Research and Quality Assurance (NCERQA). Final Report. U.S. Environmental Protection Agency, Washington, DC. April 30.

EPAORD (U.S. Environmental Protection Agency Office of Research and Development). 1989. Promotion of Scientists and Engineers in Research, Development, and Expert Positions. Chapter 5.9 in ORD Policy and Procedures Manual. ORD 5300. Office of Research and Development, U.S. Environmental Protection Agency, Washington, DC.

EPASAB (U.S. Environmental Protection Agency Science Advisory Board). 1988. Future Risk: Research Strategies for the 1990s. SAB-EC-88-040. U.S. Environmental Protection Agency, Washington, DC.

EPASAB (U.S. Environmental Protection Agency Science Advisory Board). 1990. Reducing Risk: Setting Priorities and Strategies for Environmental Protection. SAB-EC-90-021. U.S. Environmental Protection Agency, Washington, DC.

EPASAB (U.S. Environmental Protection Agency Science Advisory Board). 1994. An SAB Report: Review of MITRE Corp. Draft Report on the EPA Laboratory Study. EPA-SAB-RSAC-94-015. Science Advisory Board, U.S. Environmental Protection Agency, Washington, DC.

EPASAB (U.S. Environmental Protection Agency Science Advisory Board). 1995. Beyond the Horizon: Using Foresight to Protect the Environmental Future. EPA-SAB-EC-95-007. Science Advisory Board, U.S. Environmental Protection Agency, Washington, DC.

EPASAB (U.S. Environmental Protection Agency Science Advisory Board) 1997. Letter to C.M. Browner, administrator, EPA, on Evaluation of Research Needs for the Particulate Matter National Ambient Air Quality Standards (NAAQS) from the Clean Air Scientific Advisory Committee. EPA-SAB-CASAC-LTR-97-004. Science Advisory Board, U.S. Environmental Protection Agency, Washington, DC. March 12.

EPASAB (U.S. Environmental Protection Agency Science Advisory Board). 1999. An SAB Report: Review of the Peer Review Program of the Environmental Protection Agency. A Review by the Research Strategies Advisory Committee of the SAB. EPA-SAB-RSAC-00-002. Science Advisory Board, U.S. Environmental Protection Agency, Washington, DC.

GAO (U.S. General Accounting Office). 1994. Peer Review: EPA Needs Implementation Procedures and Additional Controls. Letter Report. GAO/RCED-94-89. U.S. General Accounting Office, Washington, DC.

GAO (U.S. General Accounting Office). 1996. Peer Review: EPA's Implementation Remains Uneven. GAO/RCED-96-236. U.S. General Accounting Office, Washington, DC.

GAO (U.S. General Accounting Office). 1999. Drinking Water Research: Better Planning Needed to Link Needs and Resources. GAO/T-RCED-00-15. U.S. General Accounting Office, Washington, DC.

Hansen, F. 1996. Memorandum to Robert J. Huggett, Assistant Administrator for Research and Development, Agency Peer Review. Office of the Administrator, U.S. Environmental Protection Agency, Washington, DC. Nov. 5.

Lock, S., ed. 1985. A Difficult Balance: Editorial Peer Review In Medicine. Philadelphia: ISI Press.

MITRE. 1994. Assessment of the Scientific and Technical Laboratories and Facilities of the U.S. Environmental Protection Agency. MTR 94W0000082V1. Center for Environment, Resources and Space, McLean, VA.

NAE (National Academy of Engineering). 1994. The Greening of Industrial Ecosystems, B.R. Allenby and D.J. Richards, eds. Washington, DC: National Academy Press. 272 pp.

NAPA (National Academy of Public Administration). 1994. A Review, Evaluation, and Critique of a Study of EPA Laboratories by the MITRE Corporation and Additional Commentary on EPA's Science and Technology Programs.

NRC (National Research Council). 1974. Report of the Review Committee on the Management of EPA's Research and Development Activities. Letter Report to EPA Administrator Russell E. Train. Washington, DC: National Academy of Sciences. Aug. 27.

NRC (National Research Council). 1977. Analytical Studies for the U.S. Environmental Protection Agency, Volume III: Research and Development in the Environmental Protection Agency. Washington, DC: National Academy of Sciences. 99 pp.

NRC (National Research Council). 1983. Risk Assessment in the Federal Government: Managing the Process. Washington, DC: National Academy Press. 191pp.

NRC (National Research Council). 1991. Rethinking the Ozone Problem in Urban and Regional Air Pollution. Washington, DC: National Academy Press. 500 pp.

NRC (National Research Council). 1993. Research to Protect, Restore, and Manage the Environment. Washington, DC: National Academy Press. 242 pp.

NRC (National Research Council). 1994a. Review of EPA's Environmental Monitoring and Assessment Program: Forests and Estuaries. Washington, DC: National Academy Press. 98 pp.

NRC (National Research Council). 1994b. Review of EPA's Environmental Monitoring and Assessment Program: Surface Waters. Washington, DC: National Academy Press. 66 pp.

NRC (National Research Council). 1994c. Science and Judgment in Risk Assessment. Washington, DC: National Academy Press. 640 pp.

NRC (National Research Council). 1995a. Review of EPA's Environmental Monitoring and Assessment Program: Overall Evaluation. Washington, DC: National Academy Press. 164 pp.

NRC (National Research Council). 1995b. Interim Report of the Committee on Research and Peer Review in EPA. Washington, DC: National Academy Press.

NRC (National Research Council). 1997. Building a Foundation for Sound Environmental Decisions. Washington, DC: National Academy Press. 87 pp.

NRC (National Research Council). 1998a. Research Priorities for Airborne Particulate Matter: I. Immediate Priorities and a Long-Range Research Portfolio. Washington, DC: National Academy Press. 195 pp.

NRC (National Research Council). 1998b. Peer Review in Environmental Technology Developmental Programs. Washington, DC: National Academy Press.

NRC (National Research Council). 1999a. Arsenic in Drinking Water. Washington, DC: National Academy Press. 310 pp.

NRC (National Research Council). 1999b. Hormonally Active Agents in the Environment. Washington, DC: National Academy Press. 430 pp.

NRC (National Research Council). 1999c. Research Priorities for Airborne Particulate Matter: II. Evaluating Research Progress and Updating the Portfolio. Washington, DC: National Academy Press. 111 pp.

NRC (National Research Council). 2000. Modeling Mobile-Source Emissions. Washington, DC: National Academy Press. 239 pp.

NSF (National Science Foundation). 1998. Grant Proposal Guide. NSF 99-2. National Science Foundation, Washington, DC. October.

NSF (National Science Foundation). 1999. Interim Report: Environmental Science and Engineering for the 21st Century: The Role of the National Science Foundation. NSB 99-133. National Science Foundation, Washington, DC. Available: http://www.nsf.gov/nsb/tfe/nsb99133

OSTP (U.S. Office of Science and Technology Policy). 1994. Technology for a Sustainable Future: A Framework for Action. U.S. Office of Science and Technology Policy, Washington, DC.

Powell, M.R. 1999. Science at EPA: Information in the Regulatory Process. Washington, DC: Resources for the Future.

Presidential/Congressional Commission on Risk Assessment and Risk Management. 1997a. Framework For Environmental Health Risk Management. Washington, DC: U.S. Government Printing Office.

Presidential/Congressional Commission on Risk Assessment and Risk Management. 1997b. Risk Assessment and Risk Management in Regulatory Decision Making. Washington, DC: U.S. Government Printing Office.

Reilly, W.K. 1993. Memorandum to Assistant, Associate, Deputy Assistant, Regional, and Deputy Regional Administrators; General Counsel; and Inspector General. Peer-Review Policy. Office of the Administrator, U.S. Environmental Protection Agency, Washington, DC. Jan. 19.

Reiter, L.W. 1999. Memorandum to Assistant Administrator Norine Noonan. Response to the Board of Scientific Counselors' Review of the National Health and Environmental Effects Research Laboratory. Office of Research and Development, U.S. Environmental Protection Agency, Research Triangle Park, NC. March 31.

Rennie, D., ed. 1990. Guarding the guardians, research on editorial peer review: Selected Proceedings from the First International Congress on Peer Review in Biomedical Publication. JAMA 263(10).

Rennie, D., and A. Flanagin, eds. 1994. The Second International Congress on Peer Review in Biomedical Publication. JAMA 272(2).

Rennie, D., and A. Flanagin, eds. 1998. The Third International Congress on Peer Review in Biomedical Publication. JAMA 280(3).

Robertson, P.D. 1999. Memorandum to Regulatory Policy Council. Sound Science and Peer Review in Rulemaking. Office of the Administrator, U.S. Environmental Protection Agency, Washington, DC. June 15.

Appendix

PAUL G. RISSER *(Chair)* is president of Oregon State University in Corvallis. Previously, Dr. Risser served as president of Miami University and provost and vice president for academic affairs at the University of New Mexico. He earned a B.A. from Grinnell College, and an M.S. and Ph.D. in botany and soils from the University of Wisconsin at Madison. He is past president of both the Ecological Society of America and the American Institute of Biological Sciences. His research interests include systems analysis of grassland ecosystems, particularly dynamics of energy and material storage and transfer, studies of vegetation structure, and natural resource planning.

JULIAN B. ANDELMAN is emeritus professor at the Graduate School of Public Health, University of Pittsburgh. He earned an A.B. in biochemical sciences at Harvard, and a Ph.D. in physical chemistry at the Polytechnic Institute of Brooklyn. Dr. Andelman's research interests have included the chemistry of trace constituents in natural waters, and modeling and measuring indoor human exposures to volatile chemicals from potable water supplies.

155

ANDERS W. ANDREN is a professor in the Water Chemistry Program and Department of Civil and Environmental Engineering and director of the Sea Grant College Program at the University of Wisconsin. He served as a member of the Science Advisory Board, International Joint Commission, and the U.S. Environmental Protection Agency Science Advisory Board. Dr. Andren earned a B.S. in chemistry from Upsala College, and an M.S. and Ph.D. in chemical oceanography from the Florida State University. His research interests include aquatic chemistry, contaminant evaporations, acid precipitation, groundwater chemistry-transport of organic and inorganics, chemical and physical property prediction, analytical chemistry of environmental microcontaminants, and contamination remediation technologies.

JOHN C. BAILAR III is a professor in the Department of Health Studies at the University of Chicago. Previously, he was chair of the Department of Epidemiology and Biostatistics at McGill University. Dr. Bailar is a member of the Institute of Medicine, a fellow of the American Association for the Advancement of Science, and an honorary fellow of the American Medical Writers Association. Currently, he serves as a member of the editorial board of the *New England Journal of Medicine*. He has served on several National Research Council committees and is a member of the NRC's Commission on Life Sciences. Dr. Bailar earned a B.A. in chemistry from the University of Colorado, an M.D. at Yale University, and a Ph.D. in statistics at American University. His research interests include research administration, biometrics-biostatistics, public health and epidemiology, and science policy.

EULA BINGHAM is a professor of environmental health in the College of Medicine at the University of Cincinnati. Previously, she served as vice president and university dean for graduate studies at the University of Cincinnati and as assistant secretary of labor for the Occupational Safety and Health Administration. She earned a B.S. from Eastern Kentucky University, and an M.S. and Ph.D. in zoology at the University of Cincinnati. Her research interests include toxicology, chemical carcinogenesis, pulmonary defense mechanisms, regulatory toxicology, and occupational and environmental health. Dr. Bingham is a member of the Institute of Medicine.

DAVID S.C. CHU is currently the vice president responsible for RAND's Army Research Division and director of the Arroyo Center. Previously, he was director of RAND's Washington Office and associate chairman of RAND's research staff. Mr. Chu is a member of the Army Science Board. He served in the Department of Defense as assistant secretary and director for Program Analysis and Evaluation. Earlier, Mr. Chu was the assistant director of the Congressional Budget Office for National Security and International Affairs. Dr. Chu earned a B.A. in economics and mathematics, and a Ph.D. in economics from Yale University.

WALTER F. DABBERDT is associate director of the National Center for Atmospheric Research (NCAR) in Boulder, Colorado. Previously, he was research scientist and manager of the Surface and Sounding Systems Facility of NCAR's Atmospheric Technology Division. He is past chair of the American Meteorological Society's (AMS) Committee on Measurements and Committee on Meteorological Aspects of Air Pollution. He has participated as a member of several advisory committees and peer-review panels for the U.S. Environmental Protection Agency. He is a member of the Editorial Advisory Board for *Atmospheric Environment* and a past associate editor of the *Journal of Atmospheric and Oceanic Technology*. In 1997, he received the AMS Editor's Award. Dr. Dabberdt earned a B.S. in meteorology and marine transportation at the State University of New York Maritime College and an M.S. and Ph.D. in meteorology at the University of Wisconsin at Madison. His research interests are in the fields of micrometeorology, air pollution dispersion, and atmospheric instrumentation.

ROLF HARTUNG is professor emeritus of environmental toxicology at the University of Michigan in Ann Arbor. He has served as a member of EPA's Science Advisory Board and on the International Joint Commission Committee on Health Effects of Water Pollution. He also served as a member of the NRC's Committee on the Future Role of Pesticides in Agriculture. Dr. Hartung received his B.S., M.W.M., and Ph.D. in wildlife management from the University of Michigan. His research interests include effects of polluting oils on waterfowl, toxicity of aminoethanols, coactions between chlorinated hydrocarbon pesticides and aquatic pollutants, environmental dynamics of heavy metals, and risk assessment.

MORTON LIPPMANN is a professor of environmental medicine and director of the Human Exposure and Health Effects Program at the NIEHS Center in the Department of Environmental Medicine and the Nelson Institute of Environmental Medicine at New York University. He also directs the EPA Center for Particulate Matter Health Effects Research at NYU. He has served as chairman of the EPA's Clean Air Science Advisory Committee and as a member of EPA's Science Advisory Board, chairman of SAB's Advisory Committee on Indoor Air and Total Human Exposure, and currently as chairman of SAB's Executive Committee. He earned a BChE degree from the Cooper Union, an S.M. from Harvard University, and a Ph.D. in environmental health science from New York University. Dr. Lippman's research is in inhalation toxicology, aerosol science and physiology, occupational and environmental exposure assessment, and air pollution epidemiology.

RAYMOND C. LOEHR is the H.M. Alharthy Centennial Chair and professor of civil engineering at the University of Texas in Austin. Dr. Loehr earned a B.S. and an M.S. from the Case Institute of Technology, and a Ph.D. in sanitary engineering from the University of Wisconsin. Previously he taught environmental engineering and had major research programs at the University of Kansas, and Cornell University. Dr. Loehr has had decades of experience related to hazardous waste management issues, the remediation of contaminated soil and sludges, and the practical application of research results. In addition, he has had major positions as chair of committees of the National Research Council, the U.S. Environmental Protection Agency, and other governmental agencies. He also is a registered professional engineer in several states.

JUDITH MCDOWELL is a senior scientist and coordinator of the Woods Hole Oceanographic Insitution's Sea Grant Program. She received a B.S. in biology from Stonehill College and an M.S. and Ph.D. in zoology from the University of New Hampshire. Her research works are in the areas of comparative physiology of marine larval and postlarval invertebrates, including studies of energetics and nutrition, coastal pollution, and the effects of pollutants on the physiology of marine animals.

DAVID L. MORRISON is an adjunct professor at North Carolina State University. He retired in 1997 from the U.S. Nuclear Regulatory Commission where he was the director of the Office of Nuclear Regulatory Research. His previous positions include technical director of the Energy, Resource and Environmental Systems Division, MITRE Corporation; president of the Illinois Institute of Technology Research Institute; and director of program development and management, Battelle Memorial Institute. Dr. Morrison has a Ph.D. in chemistry from the Carnegie Institute of Technology. His areas of expertise include research management, energy and environmental research, materials science, nuclear chemistry, physical chemistry, and the assessment of energy technologies.

GEOFFREY PLACE is retired from the Procter & Gamble Company where he held various positions, ending with vice president for research and development. He earned a B.A. and M.A. from Kings College in Cambridge, England. He is past president of the Industrial Research Institute; trustee, Children's Hospital Medical Center, Cincinnati, Ohio; and a former member of the NRC's Board on Environmental Studies and Toxicology.

BAILUS WALKER is a professor of environmental and occupational medicine and toxicology at Howard University School of Medicine. He is a member of the Institute of Medicine. Dr. Walker holds a master's degree from the University of Michigan and a Ph.D. in occupational and environmental health from the University of Minnesota, Minneapolis. His research interests are risk assessment and risk management in urban settings, including neurotoxic effects of environmental chemicals.